Modern Hebrew Poetry

Anthology of
Modern Hebrew Poetry

IN TWO VOLUMES

SELECTED BY S. Y. PENUELI

AND A. UKHMANI

Volume Two

INSTITUTE FOR THE TRANSLATION OF HEBREW LITERATURE

 AND

ISRAEL UNIVERSITIES PRESS, JERUSALEM, 1966

Israel Universities Press
is a subsidiary publishing imprint for certain books,
either published in the original language,
or translations of works not in the exact sciences,
of the
ISRAEL PROGRAM FOR SCIENTIFIC TRANSLATIONS
P. O. BOX 7145 / Jerusalem / Israel

This book has been composed in Monophoto Times New Roman at IPST,
Printed by S. Monson and Bound by Wiener Bindery Ltd.,
Jerusalem, Israel, 1966

Table of Contents to Volume Two

URI ZVI GREENBERG

1897—

Poet and publicist. Born in Bialykamien, Galicia, scion of a family of Tzadikim, *he received a traditional Jewish education. In World War I, he fought in the Austrian army on the Serbian front. His early published poems, such as* Mephisto, *were mostly in Yiddish, in which language he published an Expressionist literary journal,* Albatross, *in Warsaw and Berlin (1922-3). Settling in Palestine in 1924, he devoted himself entirely to Hebrew and contributed to the local labour press editing the journal* Sadan *('Anvil'). Drawn to the Revisionist movement in 1929, he became one of its leading intellectual spokesmen. He subsequently went to Warsaw to edit the Revisionist weekly* Die Welt, *but on the outbreak of World War II, he escaped from Poland and returned to Palestine. He was a member of Israel's First Knesset (1949-51).*

His poetry, filled with pathos and keen sensitivity, with richness of language and forceful expressions, deals with current events. It inveighs, laments and sounds a call to arms; for, according to the poet, the main function of poetry is not merely aesthetic, but rather to stir the nation to battle for its liberty. His poems deal with such themes as the significance of life and death, Israel as the Chosen People, zealous rebuttal of European culture, national pride and a vision of the restoration of the Kingdom of Israel.

His major work, Rehovot ha-Nahar *('Streets of the River') is a collection of most of his poems lamenting the European Jewish catastrophe. His Yiddish poems have been published in collections entitled* Ergetz auf Felder *('Somewhere in the Fields'),* In Zeits Roisch *('In the Tumult of Time')* Krieg oif Erd *('War on Earth'),* Varnachtengold *('Twilight Gold') and* Mephisto.

His published collections of Hebrew poems are: Emah Gedolah ve-Yareach *('A Fearful Dread and the Moon'),* Hagavrut Ha-Olah *('The Rising Heroism'),* Hazon Ahad Ha-legyonot *('A Vision of One of the Legions'),* Anacreon al Kotev ha-Itzavon *('Anacreon on the Log of Despondency'),* Kelev Bayit *('The House-Dog'),* Ezor ha-Magen u-Neum Ben ha-Adam *('The Girdle of Defence and the Speech of Ben ha-Adam'),* Sepher ha-Kitrug veha-Emunah *('Book of Indictment and Faith'),* Min ha-Hachlil u-Min ha-Kahol *('Of the Ruddy and of the Blue'),* Al Da'at ha-Nes ha Nichsaf *('The Longed-for Miracle').*

With My God the Blacksmith

In all revelations my days flare like chapters of prophecy.
Mass of metal, my flesh between them awaits the fire.
Above looms my God the blacksmith, hammering terribly.
Each wound carved in me by Time splits into a fissure,
Sparking out inward fire in flashes of memory.

My fate controls me, till day has sunk in the west.
When this battered mass, thrown back on the bed, lies still,
With a gaping wound for a mouth, which none has dressed,
Naked I say to my God: Thou hast wrought Thy will.
Now it is night: of Thy goodness, let us rest.

Translated Dom Moraes

I   Thirst for Water...

I thirst for water; wine is my need no longer,
opium no longer.
Let my brain be clear till I am that I am.
My equator—in consciousness of being.

I neighed like a colt in the sun. And joy,
even at my sandal's tip, invaded me,
brimmed at my footsteps.
Now I know: joy ever came to me
not to subtract from sorrow, but to destroy.

Now like a child I keep watch at the mirror, and see
someone there who watches me, so much resembling me.

Translated by Robert Friend

The Pole Underfoot

And this pole where my whole weight is placed:
This icy wine of joys frozen, congealed,
And the warm wet sorrow of riddles revealed—
This pole centred under all feet.

The one who feels and the one who expresses
Arrive at this point with the stream's surging roll,
With the wise man who knows and the fool who just guesses,
The one who is righteous and the one who transgresses—
Where the moon and the sun collide at the pole.

The one who is wealthy and the one who is poor;
The dreamer of dreams, the simpleton who bows—
The ploughmen in the field stop suddenly short,
For to the pole they have driven their ploughs.

And all the hunters pursuing their prey
Pause here at least once at the end of each day:
To lower their bows—

Translated by Richard Flantz

Man in Time

Man is really so deeply in time—
He is ruler over the sea and the land.
His frame is called to him with a fiery brand,
And with a swordsharp idea of meaning
He drives his lines to the stars.

But there are moments, under thick clouded bars,
Towards evening,
When he softens, discarding all plans,
For it is suddenly enough, towards evening, to nod
And to speak lyrical, old, wellworn words:
I feel so sad this evening, my God!

(And in this sadness is something that rejects going out
To seek a teller of fortunes at midnight,
To show her a hand with its secret of lines—)

Man is really as hard as the metal
Alloyed of passions as numerous as sands;
And he prides himself on the gift of his hands
In the midst of the din and the burst.

But there are times when he lifts the tips of his soul
To touch the tips of another poor soul,
To say but a word and to hear but a word—
Like a sip of live water in thirst.

Man is really so deeply in time:
His life streaming on into distances that roll,
His axe hewing the tangle of tomorrow's new goal,
But under his feet is that pole of old misery
Of the ancient, the naked, the red and the hairy,
And there is no trace of grass on the pole—

He is ready to roar: *Yah-veh!*
As once he roared.

Translated by Richard Flantz

Three Fathers

The majestic soulful prayer of Rabbi Israel of Rizhin;
His body the Scrolls of the Law in lacquered shoes, before all the
    people...
But lacquered shoes without soles, in the snow—
And the prayer of that lion of Jews, Rabbi Uri of Strelisk:
He, like a torch of fire yet not burning his clothing,
Nor moving his seat of earth with his feet—
And Rabbi Meir'l of Promishlan, he of the glorious eyes,
Who when still a boy went every market day
To learn all the animals that live, which was *kosher* and which impure,
And never let a single copper coin remain in his house overnight,
Lest a bit of metal come between him and the God of the poor...

Those are the three who rule me in time and in place:
The man of transparent stillness in the lacquered shoes,
Commanding his splendour upon me, his crowning prayer-shawl
    sweet on my shoulders—
In lacquered shoes... and the feeling of snow underfoot—
And the lion, raising a roar in the midst of his days,
Kindling my body and from it moulding words: only embers of reins;
Placing sheets of fire on my bed at night-time.
And the poorest of the poor peeping into purses and hearts
And commanding poverty upon me with bright radiant eyes:
—*Let not one copper coin remain in my house till the morning*—

Translated by Richard Flantz

Song to Heaven

Heed us when we turn our eyes to heaven
in a time of yearning, a time of sorrow,
when our yearning rises in song:
as if our daughters and we were descendants of the giants.
Once our crown was made of the gold of the sun,
and our garments, once, of the very stuff of the moon.
Mothers prepared our beds on carpets of azure
in star brightness... our childhood ages ago.
And still today we have no space for blossoming,
in which to eat our life's fruit, drink its waters,
and grind, in hard-toothed fury, our fetters into dust.
We see in our shadow's tremor the secret of our ruin.
Not the language of the low-lands is the language
of our heart, our soul, our blood;
and we breathe—alive—not the air of this present, but
—above the tree tops of the usual and all the mountain peaks of
    dailiness—
the air of our ancient days.
For in our depths there lives the song of the heavenly ones,
our shoulders tell the secret of the clipping of our wings.

Our richest resemble in this our poorest poor...
I cannot distinguish between them. I have not my life long,
neither on sea or land, for our bodies
are given to sorrow and to longing,
given to weeping... and our weeping is unto heaven.

Having vowed to remember the heavenly ones, we shall not break
  this vow
until the saviour comes, to lead us
back to our ancient greatness.

Translated by Robert Friend

Song to the Earth

We shall not lift our eyes towards the heavens—
we are not the sons of the giants nor their daughters.
Who imprinted, like a seal, on our soul this fruitless sky-yearning?
In truth, we are like trees whose roots are here... our fate is theirs:
in the joy of blossoming, the giving of fruit, in being a stump; and
   in their death
at the woodcutter's hand... As they are in the secret of the forest,
   we are in the secret of the people.

We no longer have anything in heaven... there a face is turned away—
in so much blue, so many clouds.

All that is lost, all that still exists in its truth, its grace, its needle-
   like pain,
exists here in the lower world:
here our mother conceived us, and here our father
ate the first apple;
here we milked the first goats, the baker erected his house
near the grain of the sun.
How good the bread tasted then.
Soon in this circle of bread, we, man and woman,
shall seal our life's kingdom.

Here we poured our good words, casting them into best thoughts,
myrrh and wine in a thousand songs for the blossoming of love,
here from a neighbouring, lowly rock we struck a spark of fire,
and here we raised the banners of rebellion.

Let us turn our eyes to the earth, to the mirrors of rivers and seas,
where our lost ones lie hidden, the warm ones dear to the heart,
   dear to the soul.

Here, too, lies hidden our strength's sword; and here it hacked
   to pieces
the enemy; and piece by piece we'll gather them because
in gathering there is a blessing.
And we shall cast into the melting pot
the pieces; like David, forge a sword with which to forge
a covenant with the peoples
who live by sword and spade and song.
Who seeks to destroy our blood, we shall slay him with a sword.

Here, here below are the dear, the holy, the lovely—
all the lost, for whom we shall yearn and grieve and even die.

Translated by Robert Friend

To the Mound of Corpses in the Snow

When they brought my father to the mound of corpses that was in the snow in the strange field, the German officer screamed: *'Ausziehen!'* And my father knew the verdict. My father, like one who strips from himself the substance of this world, took off his coat and his trousers, and drew off his shoes, as on the evening of the Fast of Av, and stayed standing in his white underclothes and his socks. What is more naked than such nakedness, under the dome of the sky, on that day of the universe?

In all his days, he had not stood naked in his underclothes beneath the dome of the sky, wearing on his head his black skull-cap, except at night before his bed, and in the bath-house in the moment before he entered the water to be cleansed; for then only did he take off his underclothes and his socks and remove his skull-cap: he would not look at the nakedness of his body till the water covered him all round. He entered as though to prostrate himself in the depths.

But when the officer saw that my father was still standing in his underclothes and his socks, and wearing on his head his black skull-cap, the brute struck him with his cold weapon between the shoulders and my father coughed and fell to the ground: as before God. A prostration to the depths of his being from which he did not rise. He gave a groan that was like the finishing of a last prayer, after which there is no more prayer, only a clouded sky, a heap of corpses, and a live officer, smoking in the snow-covered plain. The snow on both sides of my saintly father's face was melting, reddening, because of the blood that came out of his mouth, from his burst lungs.

And when the officer saw that my father would not get to his feet he stuck the tip of his black jackboot into the belly of my holy father, and with a kick turned him over on his back. It looked as though the earth of the Gentiles itself had kicked in my father's face.

When night fell the stars glittered, the pile of corpses lay in the field, and snow came down out of the night with soft, cruel abundance. Such was God's will. The presence of a god was felt, but of the Gentiles. There is a God in the world, but there is no god of Israel.

Only the snow was witness: it came down cruel, abundant.

Over that place my grandfather passed, the seraph, Rabbi Uri of Strelisk; whose steps made no sound there, the breath of whose nostrils left no ripple in the air. He opened his mouth and whispered,

Rabbi Chaim, the son of Rabbi Yitzhak Eliezer, my grandson,
Body that was a harp for the prayers of Israel,
Mouth which gave comfort to the oppressed heart of Israel,
How does the snow cover you in the endless field of the Gentiles?
Where did your prayers go, my grandson,
Where did my prayers go,
To what abyss in the universe...?

From out of the heap of corpses, my sister's little son, Shmuel, whom with affection they called Shmueltchy, crept: he crept to the feet of our grandfather, the seraph, Rabbi Uri of Strelisk, and cried like a child, without opening his eyes, for he could not: with the palms of his small hands he beat on the shoes of our grandfather. Our grandfather bent down and kissed his forehead and said:

'O my baby, martyred baby.'

The child of my holy sister, the little boy Shmuel, whom affectionately they called Shmueltchy, answered:

O Zeyde, Zeyde why didn't you come to us before with
thousands of angels and seraphim.

O Zeyde, where is the god of the Jews?

And the little boy was silent, lying at the feet of our grandfather,
Rabbi Uri, who had delayed coming with his firebrands, who did not
come to our house with thousands of angels and seraphim to defend
us.
Rabbi Uri of Strelisk, the seraph, knelt frozen in the Gentile field,
and snow kept falling.

Translated by A. C. Jacobs

Song of the Great Mind

That mind—the small one—is soft, like a pullet;
it is afraid of space and it loathes the dimensions of the sea;
it is a forest firefly at night,
a tavern's splinter of light in the meadow-night
to the eyes of the carter
as sluggishly through the dust he drives
horse and cart, and yawns.
Such is that mind—the small, the poor one—that serves
the peddlar on his daily rounds;
and that twistedly scorns visions of glory.
It goes through our streets near the low roofs,
licking the moss of days, drinking from drainpipes,
seeing in every cur a kind of wolf or tiger.

That mind—the great one, the one winged with light,
the supreme ruler, the high king—
(from the time the people inhabited their lands and waters,
and the king from his throne
beheld the mountains of Moab)
is not here. It sits in its nest forgotten,
but it lives. I sing to my people: Remember the eagle!
Bid it come, and it will come,
to show you
the place of passage that leads from here, the swamp of dream...
to the meaning.

So poor are we without, so twisted of shape, so shorn of all glory;
not so within the body, which is more deep

than its bodily dimensions. In it hidden lie
as in a locked palace
all kinds of marvellous and precious things,
until the tall and wide gate of the heart
is broken through by the gate-breaker
blowing a ram's horn.

Towards that day I sing; and in the hearts
of our generation, in every song,
I stir up the strife of longing. My every syllable cuts.
I catch each traitor, though disguised. I strip him bare
who teaches us to be as a reed to the river.

So poor without, such mighty lords within!
Mighty like the mountains of Lebanon,
eternal like Mt. Hermon in its snows.
And that sundering in the middle? Amen, I sing the day
on which the miraculous line of the race which Titus rent in two
will be joined.

Translated by Robert Friend

To God in Europe

[I] I'LL SAY TO GOD

God, blood has overflowed the soul; among us, the weight of his
   killed kindred
lies heavy on the head of every living creature.
And it is Sinai, it is Nevo now.
As for the *goyim,* the killers, you bless the fields of their countries,
the trees of their gardens
with a heavenly blessing. It is not they
that you have given water of gall to drink.

Who am I to add a rung to the ladder of Hebrew prayer
of my holy mother, my holy father and their children,
for whom you had no pity on that day
the *goyim* slaughtered them,
when they looked to you where you sat in heaven on high!

Where is the lost song now? Where has it streamed away?
Was it a seed sown in the lap of whoredom,
in the womb of barren time,
the burial of our soul's strong stream, the splendour of our yearning
in the soil of exile? with the corpses of the holy:
who stood in prayer in despair with the children
while the *goyim* raged midst cross and torch and spear...

God, I as one of the many beheaded of father and mother,
the heaps of whose slaughtered lie heavy upon them,
stand before you in the prayer-line of my slain ones,
I replace them in the world as a man replaces his comrade in battle,

] 264 [

lest, one link lost, their chain of eternity
drop from the hand of the living:
the chain of the race whose latest link I am,
the chain leading to me,
to the end of the day of my night, and to
the returning time of greatness,
for which the generations forged the chain.
In every circumstance, under every rule, they taught their children this,
who learned it by heart and wrote it down,
eye to eye and heart to heart.

Dumb are the slaughtered, the dust of seventy exiles stops their
    mouths:
I pray their prayer for them—and in their cadences.
Though my heart break, their Hebrew words are mine.
I believe in the continuity of this, I know completely
the earthly coast, its boundaries in dream,
where the pain of longing ends and visions wake with dawn.
In my mind I am close to all these, and I can touch them.
I am different from my forefathers: they indulged their longings,
    they prophesied right things,
but did not utter the Command of "Do" to the-people's-religion-
    of-longing.
God, therefore do I come to utter
in laws of song
this positive command,
since in Jerusalem there is not yet
ruler or commander for my people.

As I idly walk on my bounded path each day,
one of many along street and boulevard,—
the fragments of my people's disasters within me,

their weeping which is my blood,
and my legs, feelings, thoughts,
give way beneath the grave-stones of my dead—
and I walk my little path as if
I had been walking all my days
enormous distances, and in the warm flow of my blood.

I see the powerful armies of the barbarians, their wagons, chariots,
   their bolts and swords
and my intermingled tribes in the mingle of their babble:
their splendour and their darkness, the dispersal in exhaustion of
   their powers
though a bull is potent within them;
I see the brewers of mischief, the traitors, fools, sages among them:
and Satan walks among them, *but my songs, too, are among them,*
and I laugh then in my heart:
the sadness is here, true enough,
but soaring above all this, there soars the eagle of song,
carrying in his beak the crown-of-the-universal-kingdom:
All, without knowing, go
to the great palace of power,
as my will directs them,
this way or that:
in my songs is the magnet to which they are constantly drawn.

You are God, and You don't have to get
a permit to move freely around (made out in Your name)
from the Army commanders in the occupied areas,
the wide and rotting fields of Israel, Your flock.
By day the sun, at night the stars still blaze:
a bell and organ psalm of blood for the chief musician, for the
    conqueror.

Go then and move among the gentiles there,
the crosses and the dogs. They will not bark or stab or madly rage,
their ears will never hear Your foosteps' sound:
sergeant and gentile, chariot and cart, will pass as easily through You
as through the air of their street, the wind of the day, the shadow
    of a tree.

Your path is the path of a being bodiless; nevertheless,
Your vision encompasses all,
including that which is under the layers of grave-soil;
nothing is hidden, nothing can hide from you: not
six million bodies of prayer,—mind pure, heart warm with song.

You are He who knows the beginning of Abraham and the days
    of the Kingdom,
the Jews of many exiles in song.
And you know their end: that death, that terror beyond all thought,
    beyond the moulds of words;
making clear: the time has come to disperse all parchment words,
    all letter combinations
so that they stand in uncombinable isolation
as before
the giving from Mt. Sinai of the Law...

All sensible survivors of the people dwell with their grief, while I
    must gnash my teeth,
grinding words that are the children of the writ of lamentation.
But the words are not capable of expressing that deep pain when
    the need is lamentation
for every square with its item of horror in terror's mosaic.
Never before had our nation known such terror, darkening gradually
    and closing
around it, as around a tree, the ring of bereavement; and now
all light is ending. The future holds no rustle of a silken hem, no
    violin that sings
on wedding evenings in our street... About us a field teems
with graves and wells of Babylon and the streams.

Go wander about Europe, God of Israel, Shepherd-Seer, and count
    Your sheep:
how many lie in ditches, their "Alas" grown dumb:
how many in the cross's shadow, in the streets of weeping,
as if in the middle of the sea.
This is the winter of horror,
of orphanhood's sorrow, and of the fifth bereavement:
everything, everything is covered by the Christian, the silent snow
    of the shadow of death,
but not the sorrow, the orphanhood, the bereavement, the mourning,
for we have become, among the *goyim,* ashes and soap—dung for
    the dung heap.

You will count the few forsaken ones, those who have survived,
fugitive, whispering.
And they who light the smallest candle of hope in their darkness
will be heartened.
You will not cry aloud in lamentation—
God has no throat of flesh and blood, nor Jewish eyes for weeping.

And so You will return to heaven, a dumb Shepherd-Seer, after the
    shepherding and the seeing,
a shepherd staff in Your hand,
leaving not even the shadow of a slender staff on the death distances
    of Your Jews
where Your dead flock lie hidden...

A lying poet can poeticize: that after entering Your heaven
Your useless shepherd staff will shine, a rainbow in the sky.
Not I—who see within the vision the divided body of the bird.

I know very well that You will take the shepherd staff with You,
and wait till the battle subsides of Gog and Magog, who are also
    Your peoples, and our inheritors,
till the survivors assemble in the illusion of safety,
and once again there are synagogues, men praying to Your heaven,
societies again for chatter, platforms for speeches,
and again a pathway of roses for Your heretics.
And You will be the shepherd of them all.

And Jews will give their sons and daughters to the Moloch of *goyim*:
to seventy tongues—hands grasping pen, wheel, and banner;
give diligent agents of kingdoms: officers, soldiers;
give dreamers and fighters; inventors and doctors and artists;
those who turn sand into farmland and civilized landscape;
and those performing wonders—even for Albania—with their
    mastery of crafts;
give whores as well for brothels and clowns for stages,
dictionary compilers, grammar book sages
for languages still lame,
and spoken by barbarians who cannot write their name.

And there will be among us those loyal and dedicated
to all that is not ours; to the cultures that murdered us,
inherited our houses and all that they contained.
And moss will cover our racial mourning, and the sadness be hidden
of the knowledge of our people's bereavement.
Only a man like me will come with his pen in his hand
to beweep this moss-covered mourning, remembering always
the sorrow since pagan Titus's days
of an ancient race.

My rebuking pen, ripping the clouds apart,
shall make a flood descend!

Who listens to me will forsake his father and his mother and his
    friend,
he who shares his laughter and she who shares his heart,
the girl of dances and the woven wreaths—
and he will take the path my poem traces
to the lair of leopards in the mountain places.

We are not as dogs among the gentiles: a dog is pitied by them,
fondled by them, sometimes even kissed by a gentile's mouth;
as if he were a pretty baby
of his own flesh and blood, the gentile spoils him
and is forever taking pleasure in him.
And when the dog dies, how the gentile mourns him!

Not like sheep to the slaughter were we brought in train loads,
but rather—
through all the lovely landscapes of Europe—
brought like leprous sheep
to Extermination itself.
Not as they dealt with their sheep did the gentiles deal with our bodies;
they did not extract their teeth before they slaughtered them;
nor strip them of their wool as they stripped us of our skins;
nor shove them into the fire to turn their life to ashes;
nor scatter the ashes over sewers and streams.

Where are there instances of a catastrophe
like this that we have suffered at their hands?
There are none—no other instances.
(All words are shadows of shadows)—
This is the horrifying phrase: No other instances.

No matter how brutal the torture a man will suffer
in a land of the gentiles,
the maker of comparisons will compare it thus:
He was tortured like a Jew.
Whatever the fear, whatever the outrage,
how deep the loneliness, how harrowing the sorrow—

no matter how loud the weeping—
the maker of comparisons will say:
This is an instance of the Jewish sort.

What retribution can there be for our disaster?
Its dimensions are a world.
All the culture of the gentile kingdoms at its peak
flows with our blood,
and all its conscience, with our tears.

If for the Christians of this world there is
the repentance that purifies,
it is : confession. They have sinned.
They desire *the grace, the pain:*
to be Jews with a Jewish fate: the thorn bush without end—
from the king on his throne to the peasant in the field:
to raise on their staff David's banner and sign;
to inscribe the name of God on the jamb of their doors;
to banish their idols from their beautiful houses of prayer;
to place the Ark in the heart of soaring Westminster,
in St. Peter's, in Notre Dame, in every high house of God;
to wrap themselves in prayer shawls;
to crown themselves with the phylacteries
to carry out strictly the 613 commands—and to be silent:
so as not to pollute their lips with their language soaked in blood.
Perhaps their blood will then be purified, and they be Israel.

If they do not desire this with their being's full awareness,
and if they go their way—the way of Wotan and the Christian way—
a wild beast in their blood,
in the still-living-forest, night-of-beast, darkness of their heart—
then not the facade

of their courteous religiosity, the majesty of their churches,
their splendid festivals, their handsome art work,
head-halo, flower garland,
not the wonderful achievement of their best minds,
will save them
from the terrible passage
to the abyss;
not with a Jerusalem Christianity,
with such a Bible
that Wotan has not been able to digest,
so that Christianity turns in each of their bellies,
into a dish of dead sacrifice;
in every mouth, into a poisonous wine.
Wisdom and conscience sink within those rising vapours;
all notions of compassion
(as with the journeymen of scaffolds)
are confounded.

Either Wotan, the forest, the spit, the axe,
the roasted, bleeding limbs of the living;
or Sinai, the Tablets of the Laws, the God of Israel.

Wotan and Christianity are the secret of the disaster!
The world does not know.

[IV] THE JEWS AND THE BEAST

The feeling:—God, Father in Heaven, gracious Lord and Defender,
on the wheel of time between twilight and twilight—
doesn't exist in the heart of a beast,
doesn't exist in the beat of its heart.
Because its fate in the beautiful world is—to be killed;
although not given the knowledge of its fate,
but possessed of the knowledge of fear.
And it isn't its body that casts a shadow,
but the constant fear that is its shadow.
It trembles at the shadow of itself;
nor is its sleep secure.
This is its whole existence in the world.
In this it resembles a Jew in the world.
This is his fate when the gentiles attack him.
Melancholy comes with the ripples of wind;
with the trembling of fish in river waters;
with the gathering of clouds over trees of the forests.
Shivers of fear with every rustle, knock, or cry,
from every side, from every human tread.

There is no man in the world so sad as a Jew in the evening,
and none so sad as a beast in the evening...
and there is no man like a Jew who weeps and cries out
in the fear of his dream in the night—

God is not the beast's gracious Lord and Defender;
therefore it is killed
thus, openly, a murder sanctioned,
to the wrath and the joy of the killer!
And in this the Jew in the world resembles it.

] 274 [

Yet it was he who discovered God in the world!
In the fate of the beast—the fate of the Jew...
But in his heart a multitude of feelings, the warmest idiom,
a combination of precious letters notated for prayer,
a taste of honey and milk in his mouth from the song of his king,
the good longing,
the lofty prayer,
the warm tear
that purifies...
And there was a god who was a father, prodigal of mercy and power;
    a shield; and full of grace
as if it were possible to say that the half light of morning and evening,
and the whispers of the shining ones round the height of the world in
    the sky,
no longer bear witness to the existence of God.
Did my dead, did my incinerated know, when they stood before the
    goy before their death,
that their whole life till then between twilight and twilight
had been utterly betrayed
through a fantasy of faith, more powerful than the knowledge of
    knowers,
in which longings put on branches, put on wings, and struck
    enormous roots
to the depth and width of their bodies?
Did my dear ones know that Jews have no father in heaven to defend
    them,
as they have no defending armies and fortresses on earth?
that vain was the good longing,
vain the warm tear
and the lofty prayer,
vain the combination of precious letters notated for prayer
in summer and winter and spring

all the days of their life in the world?—
Did they know that theirs was the fate of a beast?
What language can express the horror of this knowledge suddenly
    there in the world
in those last moments before Hell—

But my unhappy Muse,
not this... not this horrifying knowledge is the essence of horror!
"You are happy, beast," says the poet who is wrong.
You were never—like a Jew—led to the scaffold fully aware!
You were never ordered by your murderers to dig with your own
    hands
a grave for yourself!
You were never shoved into the crematories with your mother and
    your father and your children!
You are happy, beast, because you had woods and holes to hide in.
and safe corners in houses!
But not the Jews,
who resemble the gentiles in the shape of their bodies, in their clothes,
    in the color of their white skin,
in the red of their blood...
They didn't have a wood to escape to, a tree for shade, a hole to
    hide in!
The cats of the Jews and the dogs of their yards,
the birds on the roofs or in their nests,
the buzzing flies and the butterflies
remained after them,
and the Jews—do not exist!

[v] GOD AND HIS GENTILES

It wasn't for nothing that Europe's faithful Jews
did not raise their heads
to study with their eyes the pride of her cathedrals,
the beauty in them: arch and spire and carving.
As if seared by their shadows the faithful Jews went by them—
not for nothing, not for nothing!
We know this clearly now.
From within them the horrors came
and came upon us.

If God in Europe should descend
to the thresholds of cathedrals
and ask His Christians, those who enter there
to pray to Him and praise Him:
"Where are My Jews?
I do not hear their voices in the heavens,
and therefore have I come to seek them here...
What is the meaning of their sudden silence?
Where have they disappeared?
Has there been an earthquake?
How is it then
That they've been swallowed up and you survive?
And if the beasts came from their forest to devour men
and ate them only, sparing you
are they then so wise?
You have raised up in the city to My glory
splendid cathedrals—
and if in My name you have raised them,
your God stands on your threshold.
Where then are My Jews?"
The gentiles would answer fearlessly:

"There were Germans here and we saw eye to eye.
We killed them. All your Jews,
old and young alike!
We killed them, sparing them no horror,
until they left a space,
as the felling of trees in a forest leaves a clearing.
We had hated them for so many years,
ever since you were nailed to the cross, Pater Noster!
And thought You hated them as much.
Thus, from our childhood, had we been taught
by father, priest, and book.
We saw as well that You had given us field and rulership,—
them, not even the shelter of the sky.
They were the vulnerable. The despised. The to-be-trodden-on.
And then the German came and said: "Among you there are many
Jews.
Let us make an end to them.
And this is the end, Pater Noster!"
And then, leaning His back against the gate,
God would look at his Christians—
voiceless, speechless.
And the gentiles would see in Him the likeness of a Jew:
wild ear-locks, a beard like a mane before Him,
the very eyes of a Jew;
and see that the cathedral resembled a synagogue,
and that there was no cross now at the entrance.
And the Christians would roar like beasts of the forest:
"Is there still one Jew left among us?
Does a synagogue still stand in our city?
Hey, boys, let's start a little fire.
We'll need kerosene, crowbars, axes."

Translated by Robert Friend

Song of My People-Forest People-Sea

When a man walks in the forest and lifts his voice there,
the great forest answers with an echo-echo,
a sign that the voice has entered and shaken its forest heart;
but when a man wanders the sea and lifts his voice to the sea,
the sea never answers, the water goes on flowing...
Like the voice of a man on the open sea, such is the voice of the seer
in my-people-that-are-a-sea... my people-sea! in the manifold world.

But my people-sea, who are a sea for all their seers,
are a forest everlasting for the peoples of the world:
giving the best of wood for pillars and sills
and roofs of palaces;
cloud after cloud will be sent on the head of my people-forest
to the alien nations; they will come
to lay the trees low. There the beasts of prey assemble.
When an alien people rise beyond my forest-people and lift their voices,
my people-forest will answer them!
Not so when a prophet and seer with powerful voice stands up from
    within them,
and where he stands, there is the heart of the sea... my people-sea!

In truth, a curse of generations, a sin of generations...
a sadness not even madness can overcome!
Is it of God, this cruelty?

Happy the innocent or fool, happy the man, ignorant of the heart
    of this,
like the blind and deaf harper when his hands are on the strings,

like the man who walks, led by imagination's miracle,
behind a plough in the heart of the sea,
and thinks: a field! and ploughs furrows in the waters;
a field! and casts seed upon the waters...
But woe unto the seer-sage who knows the secret,
a fear in his luminous mind
until his mind trembles, a torch in the wind...

He knows that this is a sea and not a field
but walks on the sea and he ploughs and sows:
Perhaps a miracle will happen; and the cruel god
of generations, leading a desert wind, will bid the sea to be
a continent;
the sea and the waves of the sea turn field and its fat furrows,
and that which was sown in it in the knowledge of a longed-for miracle
rise green and golden,
every grass according to its kind, every tree, and all the grains of the
     sun.

All my days and all my nights are a prayer for the miracle.

Translated by Robert Friend

For the Tearing of the Mind

Here are my brothers, the money-changers, the pedlars,
whose life goes on forever.
The Temple Guards are gone, but these remain.
And here is the rubble of the ruined Hebrew Temple—
and on the rubble, made of solid marble,
a temple of crescents for Arabia's prayers.
Here are my cousins, here the braying of donkeys,
and here the excrement of sheep and men...
This is the city of David!
In all the caves of the city
there is no prophet, a tiger on his knees...
but Arab, Jew and gramophone.
And this is the Prison Court, where the prophesying lion
was thrown, to be consumed by his own fire.
When was this?
Ask anyone who urinates against this wall.
Ask.
And this the Valley of Gehenna, where they brought
the sinless babes to Moloch.
And this the blocked Gate of Mercy,
which will split open
stone by stone
when the Messiah knocks at the Mount of the Temple.
I shall not see his coming. Here
on the Mount of Olives opposite, on this slope then,
I shall be crumbling bones.
There is no balm for searing of the heart,
the tearing of the mind,

the conscience blazing,
till the legs fail and cannot bear the body
away, away from here,
so that it will not fall, a camel groaning,
before the money-changers, the pedlars and the cousins.

Translated by Robert Friend

AVRAHAM REGELSON

1896—

Poet and critic. Born in White Russia, he emigrated with his family at an early age to the USA, where he attended yeshiva *and later taught. He lived in Palestine from 1934-37, and in 1949 settled permanently in Israel, where he worked on the editorial staff of* Am Oved *publishing house, and later on that of the* Al Hamishmar *daily.*

His poetry, intellectual in character, tends to romanticism, symbolism and the abstract, and is prominently concerned with a moral element. It takes the form of an intellectual epic myth: the world is revealed as a manifestation of biological, eternally reproductive forces; in the development of man and nature, the desire for survival, conquest and creation clashes with the negative, destructive instincts. The development of the world is, in effect, a constant process of rebuilding on ruins. His imagery is monumental, garnered from both the inanimate and the living world, from plant and animal life, from man and from the universe as a whole.

Cain ve Hevel, a poem dealing with the eternal clash between violence (Cain) and spiritual force (Abel). Hakukot Otiotayikh *('Engraved are Thy Letters') a paean to the Hebrew language.*

Collected verse: El ha-Ayin ve-Nivka *('Non-being Cleft').*

Collected essays and reviews: Melo ha-Talit Alim *('A Robeful of Leaves') and* Sham ha-Bedolah *('There is the Crystal').*

He has translated into Hebrew works of Greenwood, Kipling, Herman Melville, William Blake, Walt Whitman and others.

Anent the Man of the Stars

[I]

As of old, the Sea with unceasing roar rolls
  its blue hillocks,
Heaving and shattering them against the shore
  in turbulent hem of foam,
And the bougainvillea blossoms cling dusty purple unto
  the houses of the youngling city
And carob and sycamore survivals, bowed with age,
  splotch the gleaming sands;
The morning Sun washes crystalline the cubes
  of the workers' quarter in the north,
And Jaffa's elbow, red-sprinkl'd, juts out into the water
  where near the painted vessels ride;
And clear, clear is the skybell conching all.
But in the very white of daylight a weird dunness falls,
For plugg'd is a man's heart,
Stricken one precious of mankind,
A man—heart of a Nation named heart,
A lov'd one and brother and father,
Unto me and unto ye a father,
An envoy of the Stars who walked about among us,
Cloth'd in his grey cloak, bearing his crook-headed cane,
His eyes forth-welling amberlight and lovingness,
His sorrow-wrinkles kindling in smiles,
One good, good-doing, loyal,
By his mouth's grace vivifying the wisdom of generations
And on his shoulders the burdens of generations lading,
One awake, asinging, vibrant, luminous,

] 285 [

And lo! he was eras'd and reft,
And the cycle of days revolves and runs without him.

[II]

Very lonely was he
Though his flesh was bathed in your odour
And his affection confiscate to all in need.
Bury him in his loneliness atop a mountain
In sight of the mass'd people standing below,
And let the morning-star beam on him
And morning-birds sing above him in boughs of
   cypress and pine, guarding his headboard.
Lay no flowers on his casket,
Neither flag nor prayer-shawl—
Simple was the man,
Far from vacuous ornament and the trappings of piety,
And in his simpleness
Lower him into the soil he loved.
And it came to pass, no sooner did his body-remains reach the gate
   of the Jewish city
When amid sweat and crowding and noise
He was brought unto a close-press'd community grave.
Rapped the clods six dull thuds on the casket,
And instead of the warm flesh,
   lavish of mercies, emanative of understanding,
Remained for the eye a patch of red dust
Saturate with a broken widow's tear.
Weightier her tear than all our summèd tears!
For, while we as despoilers came
To take—one a breath of love, one a crumb of learning,
Another a hand-strengthening word,
And still another, delusive self-honouring,

She cleaved unto the creature-life of him.
Guarded and defended and maintained,
Overtented him from youth till old age,
And of a sudden he was snatched from her,
And shatter'd, pulveriz'd is her world.

[III]

In the deep of night,
When city-noise is hush'd
And starlight waxes strong,
And the echo of my measur'd footstep is heard
   against the muffl'd moan of the sea,
I invoked within my soul the square of red dust,
Bent unto it an inner ear,
And lo! silence there, not a hint, not a spark
   from the casket hidden underneath.
Is this the all of the man, a little ash, a little rot?
And what to him is all the depth quarried in his works,
And what the beauty which had crown'd his thoughts,
And what to him all the praise and the lament
   accorded him after his passing?
And behold! I sensed the patch of dust expanding,
Blending with the entire ball of Earth,
And Earth sang and danced beneath me.
Marvelled the Stars,
And in language of tremblings and emotions
Which aye stretch from body unto body
   and conjoin worlds
(For only to our senses, lovers of the
   solid and what may be grasp'd in hand,
Is there sunderance between thing and thing),
The stars said to her:

"What is thy joy, O Earth,
And why this day of all days dost dedicate a dance?"
And Earth to them made answer:
"From me came forth, in me did live,
And unto me today returned
A man of wonders, a kenner of me and ye,
A breather of my grasses and my rains,
A hearkener unto the prayer of my birds,
One who my life by his life did augment.
Like an artist, rejoicing over a chapter completed in purity,
So do I rejoice.
For each man and folkstem, and mankind entire, and every
    family of animal and plant,
Are a chapter in my interfolding scrolls,
A swirl, a flow, in the sea of my life,
For a while welling out of me
And in me re-swallow'd,
And each change and tremor passing them,
Not in barrenness doth pass
But cometh to enhance my soul, and all of us to glorify.
Seek ye among the planet-bands
If ever was one like to him,
A supernal rose of intellect
Blooming and shining before your eyes—
His thought embraced eternities;
Concentrated in his brain,
Time, Space and Nature about their own being wondered,
Their own beauty relished.
At one he was with creeping thing and
    bud of grass,
With sea-compelling moon and
    silent song of stars—

Genius I gloried in,
First fruitage of my wombing.
No Firstborn but is a sacrifice,
Slaughtered daily at rise and at set,
Lash'd by lightning-pains to go forth and shine,
Though ruin'd be his temples,
Though he sorely tirèd be.
And he with joy did bear his fire and wood,
With love did give his whole self
    to engender and to nourish,
Co-agent in our cryptic tasks.
Sing ye now with me together,
Approve his beingness,
Praise ye his birth and his death
For one moment are these,
One decree and one necessity
    in the heart of Existence.
And thou, Nation scatter'd throughout all my climes—
    for carv'd he was of thee
    and thy longings he spake forth,
By his merit be thou enmeritèd,
Gather him into the treasury
    of thy visionaries great,
Thy life-sustainers
    from thousand generations unto thousand generations;
And chant for him a chant of
    thanksgiving and exaltedness,
A labour-chant, a psalm of betrothal unto thy Chosen Soil,
A hymn of behusbanding the Land, and its pregnancy,
And fruit of splendrous futurities,
To slake the anguish of man, and my yearning innernesses,
    and the thirst of the Stars in their multitude."

] 289 [

Earth ceased.
A large bat in wide sweeps
   wheeled on the outskirts of a streetlamp glow,
And a cricket strummed his thin fiddle
   against the growing tumult of the Sea.

[IV]

The Nation has its comfortings,
But for me, for ye—the lack and the grief.
Vast is my longing for you, Bialik!
Not again shall I see you walk in the street,
   your hand in blessing on a stripling's shoulder
   and your talk sweet in his ears;
Not again shall I see you at evenfall, in shadow, silent,
Embroidering a veilèd thought, gazing through
   your window at the hills in Ramat Gan;
Not again to my sight will you thrust your nose into a book,
   hungrily cropping its yield;
Not again shall I behold your face at a colleagues' meet
   on a drizzly day, drab in your overcoat, your lips
   slightly open in wonderment, and the grooves of
   your forehead—lovable.
Too frail am I to bear even a flimsy portion
   of your burden,
Too slight am I to onward-spin the thread of
   Israel's Shekhinah-life, upheld
   and procreated by your song.
A sawn-off sycamore branch, storm-stricken and raggèd,
   cast upon the sands,
Let the Sea take me where it will.
On an alien shore
Some few nights will I shine in my decay,

Until the merciful mud shall cover me.
But, through Genesis-layers, and lavas which
   remember Sun's birth,
Through river-veins hidden under mountain-roots,
Shall pass a shiver and a thrill,
Shall run a throbbing between the ash of my body
   and the dust of your body,
(For that my lips in faith had touched your hand);
And in the august logic of the Earth
   and the rhythm-reckoning of the Stars,
Beyond all my squalor,
I shall know your light as one of your sons
   in Eternity.

Translated by the author

YITZHAK LAMDAN

1900—1950

Poet, essayist and publicist. Born in Vohlin, Russia, he was a World War I refugee, joined the Russian Army during the Karensky Revolution, and witnessed the Ukrainian pogroms. In 1920, he settled in Palestine and worked as a road and farm labourer.

His poetry, expressionist in nature, is wholly devoted to the fate of the Jewish people at its decisive hour. His major poetic work Massadah *expresses the struggles of the Third Aliya: their realistic and ideological world of yesterday has gone up in the flames of the diaspora, and they strive to build up a new way of life in their homeland amidst hardship and tribulation, hope and despair. His other collected verse—*BeRitmah Meshuleshet *('Treble Harness'),* Misefer Hayamim *('From the Book of Days'),* BeMaaleh HaAkrabim *('Scorpions' Rise)—express the harsh fate of the Jewish people, subject to the destiny imposed on them by God; they voice a call to the national conscience, amidst gloomy forebodings.*

Lamdan published the literary monthly Gilyonot *and other periodicals for twenty years. He translated into Hebrew works by Max Brod, D'Annunzio, Michailis, Conrad, Jack London and others.*

Myths Told Me

On an autumn night, on a bed of sorrows, far from home and
    shattered hearth,
My mother died;
A last tear froze in her eyes as she gasped a dying blessing
To me, her son, setting forth for far-off alien fields of battle,
An army kitbag weighing down my back...
On grave-studded pain-packed Ukrainian roads
My soft-eyed innocent brother fell,
And did not find a Jewish grave.
My father alone remained by the doorpost rising from the ashes
    of ruins,
Weeping a lonely prayer on the ravaged scroll of God.
And I—
Girding my disintegrating soul
With final words of courage
Fled at midnight to a ship of exiles
To ascend Massada.

Myths told me:
There the last banner of revolt is raised,
Calling to heaven and earth, to God and man:
"Reparation!"
And on tables of rock stubborn nails
Scratch a message of consolation;
There a breast of dissent is bared, roaring
Against a hostile fate of generations:
"Strife!
Me or you!

Here battle will pass the last judgment
On life!"

Myths told me:
Among Massada's walls walk prophets
Prophesying redemption,
And in the tents among the paths are Levites,
Singing "To the Chief Musician"
And the echo of tomorrow answers them:
"Amen, Selah!"
There, from the summit of the wall, flowers of priesthood
Raise arms of compassion
To the wretched sky of orphaned night,
Praying that its flawed moon wax full and bright...

Myths told me:
Over the heads of the fighters
A spirit has descended, weeping in atonement,
And through the curtain of the future a great eye of dawn looks out
And watches over Massada.

Translated by Richard Flantz

Tender Offering

And who are you ascending here so gay,
With dewdrops on your head?
—Not dewdrops—they are tears
A loving father and mother shed
On the head of their only son
As he went away.
My mother sobbed and my father wept:
"Where will you go, and you still so tender,
So tender and soft?"
And I hardened my heart:
"And what of it?
A tender offering shall be accepted!"
And I went
And so I ascend in joy,
And though there be tears on my head—
I am happy and rejoice!
I know, my father and mother weep bitterly now
Into the palms of trembling hands,
And I love them, I love them so...
But the myth of Massada is so lovely
And the wall of wonders so alluring—
If father and mother knew the myth
They would not weep that their only son
Is gone towards it!...

Translated by Richard Flantz

The Hands of Israel

And who are you, ascending with your hands outspread?
—Not mine! They are the hands of Israel, that embrace everything,
And everything tumbles out of their embrace,
And they hang like empty pails
Over the world's overflowing wells...
Ah, these hands, the first to raise the banner of any revelation,
And the last to gain its solace,—
Are lately raised towards Massada's walls—
To embrace!
I charge you, hands of Israel, if from here too you return empty—
Then fumble in empty space!
I charge you to grasp Massada's walls,
To grasp them unrelenting!
Or else-may these hands be cut off from whose embrace
Everything tumbles,
Whose grasp grips nothing!

Translated by Richard Flantz

The First Fruits

With song and drums, laden with all goodly things, let us ascend
   the wall,
Bringing as gifts hands filled with hearts golden in dreams,
Bearing pitchers of youth flowering with blood that sings,
And early clusters of life in baskets of love—
All as an offering to the battle and sacred to Massada!
O wall! Open up the gates of your empty crypts
And store the crops of our lives for the years of battle,
For still Massada's fields lie barren and sword-battered,
And who knows how much longer the battle and siege may last!
So till the good years come, and rains fall in their seasons,
And dew drops down each night on unfortified earth,
Until the scythe of victory reaps the blessings of the field securely—
Accept the first fruits of our lives, to feed your hungry fighters,
And the wells of our youth—for those who thirst!

Translated by Richard Flantz

Prayer

As for those who escaped foreign gallows and ascended the wall—
Guide their steps, O God, lest they stumble, or fall,
For they are feeble still, and weary.
And for those whose suns have grown dark in the world's seven
    heavens—
Grant, O God, the grace of Massada's last sun,
For if this too grows dark—where then shall they turn?
And to those who burst the swaddling banners of seventy nations—
Give O God a shirt to warm them and cover them,
In their trembling beaten nakedness...
As for those whose mother's milk has not yet dried upon their lips
And on whose cheeks the warm caress of father's hand still flutters—
Ease, O God, their orphanhood, be their father and their guard,
Lend their tender arms the strength to hold a heavy shield,
Soften Massada's hard rocks as pillows for their weary heads!
And for those who in tears have sown here the seed of soul and
 dreams—
Let not the seed be struck by the hail of grief, nor dried by sudden
drought,
Command, O God, many rains of solace, many nourishing dews of
    night,
Till it grow to reap reparation!
As for those who breached the wall and came with ashes of destruction
    on their heads
And mourning sackcloth round their hips, to win consolation in this
    battle—
Lend them perseverance, God, when consolation is long in coming!
And to those on whom the nation's spirit has laid the riddle of its fate,

The task of providing solutions, of leading it to open gates—
Give strength, O God, and courage, to bear this heavy burden
Up to the border that in a last vision the afflicted spirit saw!...
Weary, weary are Massada's sons, the suffering of these few is heavy.
And those who survived many battles, baring breasts to every arrow,
Have one more battle to survive, this long and stubborn battle
For this single strip of land-
Feast their spirits, God, extinguish not the flames of revolt
They brought as holy Sabbath candles to the wall
At the twilight of the worlds.
As night descends upon the wall—do not let the fires die!
From darkening horizons loneliness rises and threatens,
Satiety walks among the paths, whispering in every ear,
And weary ears incline, absorb the steady whisper...
Yesterday's memories weaken arms, and heads, always erect
And leaning forwards, are bent back in weariness;
Vain dreams spread dread and deep confusion among the fighters;
The sickle of misery reaps, and many, many are the fallen.
Spare them, O God, for the battle—why must these despairs come too
Upon Massada and its fighters?
Why should all the stars burn out when on the wall the fires die,
And one star alone remain—Israel's nightmare-star?—
Blazing seventyfold in ghastly light, sowing terror, its rays
Piercing the cracks in the walls, lighting up the chaos outside,
Ah, again and again the chaos———
How long will the emaciated hand of a nation
Fumble with blind fingers on the locks of salvation?
O God, look, the hand is stretched forth,
Between sea and wasteland it is stretched forth,
In its palm a last dream grown meagre from nights of restless
   wandering:
MASSADA!

] 301 [

To the numbered dead upon the wall this dream and its solution are
   given.
If this time too you have no mercy, God, and the dream is not
   accepted,
And this time too the sacrifice of those who solve it is not respected—
God, guard Massada!

Translated by Richard Flantz

Jonah Flees from the Presence of His God

> *But Jonah rose up to flee unto Tarshish*
> *from the presence of the Lord... and*
> *the Lord sent out a great wind into*
> *the sea, and there was a mighty tempest...*
>
> Jonah, 1 :3-4.

You have found me, my God! Between sea and sky your tempest
 impales me.
No, I did not ask if a man could flee his shadow, or if a tree
Could command its roots: "Release me, sons of darkness,
And I, the trunk, shall wander far away from you, alone!"
But now I know: Along one road alone is a man led to his destiny,
And though seventy-seven times he flee his fate—he shall not escape.

I said: This man will lie down and sleep in the sides of the ship:
No, not the son of Amittai, too weak to bear his truth;
Not Jonah, whose innards burn like a flaming growth, his burden
And his vision like a howling herd of jackals spreading terror over him—
But a man without yoke or burden, without two worlds, two lives:
A living heap of dust and ashes on the calmly floating cradle of the
 waves,
A man whom nothing angers, who can look upon men and nations
As one would look at stars that move unchanging in their circuits.
And now your storm has caught me up! And I do not know who
 rages more—
My heart trapped in the palm of your hand or this wildly frothing sea
That now destroys the ship because it gave shelter to the man
Who from his mother's womb was dedicated to shelterlessness.

] 303 [

God, my God, my pursuer, why have you fallen thus upon me?
Answer me—what did I take, what was missing after my flight?
Why do you scourge me? Have I stolen the key of the universe?
Will the sun not come and go on time without me,
And will the sounds of the world be stilled with the stilling of my
  words?
Will the earth cease to bring forth its yield and the trees to bear their
  fruit
If I do not bear my burden?
Why do you pursue me? From the mouth of every wave your voice
  roars out to me:
"Return and prophesy, Jonah, return and preach my-word-your-word!"
No! I shall not return, my God! I have sworn to speak no more!
I shall flee! Even knowing that my pursuer and impaler is within me!
I shall fly far from my land, no longer willing to be a man between:
Between God and man, between earth and sky,
A constant target for the arrows of both!
I am no longer willing to be flung between the two as in a sling,
Not knowing of which of the two I am and why I am between them,
Without the grain of the earth or the grace of heaven!

I am no longer willing to be unwilled, unwished for upon your earth,
This earth from which I was taken, this earth which I have loved.
Release me! And if in your eyes I am disgraced for having gone
  against you,
Then who am I that this tempest should rise because of me? And why
Is my rebellion of such value that the chasms of the sea should gape
And rage around it and the army of waves should pound?
And if I am dear to you—why not let me go free, my God,
Free of your burden which must bend my life and drag me down
By its heavy weight into the heaving depths?
I shall not return. I shall not be again what I have been

] 304 [

Since the day you laid your hand upon me!
And if I be cast out and it be said: "Blinded is Jonah's vision,
And the spirit of the Lord is gone from the son of Amittai!"—Why,
I shall rejoice! For are not they who so cast me out the same
Who only yesterday, as I was preaching in their midst, mocked me,
    saying:
"Why does this phrase-drunk mumbler force his lips to labour?"
How I scorned their mockery and their mercy as an abomination and
    a stench!

And Nineveh—all her wickedness upon me? Let her sin to her heart's
    content!
I never tasted the wine of her sins, though thirsty and famished
I walked through her streets when her table of evil brimmed with
                    variety—
I did not even touch a crust of the bread of her charity!
I knew her charity! As a horse, weary from running, retreats and slows
Its pace that it may plunge into a quicker gallop,
So Nineveh will retreat from her sins, that tomorrow she may add
And redouble sins for every single sin of yesterday.
Let Nineveh sin, let her live, let her be merry, let her lose herself
    in sin!
Is that not her law? Is that not why she was made?
And I have had enough of being a stumbling-block that cannot block
An unshakable law of the world!
I have sworn that I shall not return, my God! Is there not,
Among the secret places of your world, a hiding-place and sanctuary
For me as well, when there are towns of sanctuary
For every murderer and killer?
And why will you deny sanctuary to a man who killed his inner peace
And threw the pieces to people who did not want it?
Is there no corner, my God, where I can nestle like a tree of the field,

With the living silence of your light above and the darkness of your
    earth beneath
Where I can bow my head at times to your changing winds and rains?

Is there not, among the stones of your fields, a stone on which
I may rest my head at evening, to the echoing pulse of retreating day,
And fall asleep without horrifying dreams or dreadful visions of the
    future?
Let me go and I shall flee there, to that view where I will know no
    more,
Know nothing—except the grace of passing away and the gleaning of
    grapes.
Oh, leave me alone! Each rising frothing wave is like a giant's arm
Raised upon me in wrath to catch me and to bring me back,
But I am determined: I shall not return, my God!
Rise, tempest! Swell! Wrap me round and sweep me down into the
    depths
Like an unwanted trampled clod of earth, like an unknown seaman
    drowned!
Let the waves vent their rage upon me, let the vast abyss swallow me,
Let me never return to land as Jonah, son of Amittai,
Servant of God and his truth, bound to the wake of his glory
As it trails in the dust of the earth.

Translated by Richard Flantz

Psalm of Love and Hate

What I have loved in you, great rock whence I was hewn,
I shall wear like a precious robe embossed with glorious sheen,
And what I've hated in you I shall wear beneath,
Like prickly sackcloth that combs my flesh unseen.

What I have loved in you, lonely rock whence I was hewn,
Will shine like all eternity in a young boy's eyes,
And what I've hated in you will flash its terror through me
Like the fearful flash of a knife raised for sacrifice.

What I have loved in you, my trunk of heavy ages,
Will play upon my hours like unseen hands on keys,
And what I've hated in you will wail and howl within me
Like the howl of homeless dogs on a night of rain and freeze.

What I have loved in you, my trunk of dark confusion,
I shall carry like a promise, like the smile of the autumn sun,
And what I've hated in you in my heart I'll ever carry
Like a dagger buried in it deep within.

What I have loved in you, my source, my lord, my God,
Is too much to be weighed by the weights of any nation,
And what I've hated in you is too dark to be illumined
By the single sun, this world's sole illumination.

What I have loved in you shall yet be put up as a sign
On all the doorposts of the future, my source so cursed and hounded,
And what I've hated in you, Oh God of the fear of Isaac,
Lead me on to the future without it, without it!

Translated by Richard Flantz

] 307 [

The White Revelation

Ah, first white of temples gleaming in the glass—
So comprehended and beyond comprehension!
Why, O skull, do you wag your mane of dissent?
You won't shake off the pass
Of the seed that obeys
The white revelation!

Ah, white of temples, white like the flag of peace
Held by one forced to surrender
To whoever rises against him,
To the here and the yonder,
To what is over and past,
And to what approaches apace—
His enemy and host...

Ah, silvering temples, suddenly, at times,
You gleam with such a cold terrifying blaze,
Like the steel flame of a sword drawn from its sheath,
That the eyes close and cease from their gaze,
And sights of forgotten climes,
Of a distant land of cold,
Unfold beneath
Their lids:

Wide expanses of snow-steppe, glaring white,
Where a single speck of black appears:
The passing sled—
Its bells echo sadly in the ears

As with pounding hoofbeats and lashing whip
It fades into the infinite
White of distance
And is swallowed up.
And again nothing remains in sight
Except the snow-steppe,
Cold—and whitest white.

Ah, first white of temples gleaming in the glass—
Such a sudden gleam of fright!
Why, O my skull, do you wag your mane of dissent?
You can't shake off the pass
Of your victor's hand
So cold and white!

Translated by Richard Flantz

Ballad of the Other I

His soul is a wheel of changes on the axle of Unrest,
To which henceforth and onward his eyes are ever drawn;
In each revealed opaqueness he seeks the hidden spyhole,
And from the shore of true solutions, sails off to the unknown.

An exit to another entrance he seeks at every entrance,
Each yoke that appears before him is a vision to detest;
Of all the words and idioms that men speak on this earth,
He loves the wondrous parable, the riddle and the quest.

His slightest move is a fluttering—of lidded wells of distance,
The lightest wave of his hand—an oar, pulling who-knows-where;
He was my soulmate, he; I saw into all his visions,
And when I was yet a boy, all my love with him I shared.

To a secret land of nowhere and to a legend with no name,
He took along my longings on a distant endless voyage,
And on the masts of all my days, hung them out as banners calling
To a place where the heart forgets all duty, law and bondage.

From out the hives of dread that darken human destiny,
The sad juice-heavy honey he taught me to suck dry,
And in every cloud of agony, the rainbow of peace he showed me—
I loved him, yes, I loved him—once he was I—

Once he was I. When was it? And was it ever so?
He seems like some strange image, from out a fantastic plot,
Ever since I sent him from me, and put my life into the yoke
Of a generation in dissent with nations and with God.

Like a distant dream I see him, a dream both good and bad,
Since I turned my back upon him to join in covenant and deed
With a land of poisoned fate, hard of spirit and of vision,
Where every path—bridle in hand—is vicious cruel need.

Now he steals in every day, and knocks upon my door,
And I shrink back and shudder, and do not call: "Come in!"
I fear his very glance, his speaking and his silence,
The wisdom and contentment of his frank confiding grin.

And every night as well, he peeps in through my window,
With eyes that speak his plea: "Open up and let me in!"
And I turn my face away, harden my heart, ignore him,
And I know now that the miracle can never occur again.

I tremble at his coming: can I look him in the eyes,
When I have killed my love, stifling its very echo?
He will not understand me, his eyes are all for distances,
And what is here close-by, he'll never see or know.

He will not know that there's an agony heavier than taking wing,
And a yoke that's so much vaster than the freedom of expanses,
And a mighty revelation, whose every leaning shadow
Darkens the wells of distance and their suggestive glances.

He will not understand: There is a duty
That can make a man turn cruel to those he holds most dear;
I will understand his speech, he will not fathom mine—
And so I dread his coming, and his tempting words of cheer.

] 311 [

So he'll go on knocking on my door and peeping in my window,
Lurking like an unseen shadow from which I cannot hide,
And I, as if unhearing, I do not call: "Come in!"
I am as if unseeing, and my heart is there outside.

Translated by Richard Flantz

AVRAHAM SHLONSKY

1900—

Poet. Of Ukrainian birth, he came to Palestine to study in 1913, lived in Russia during World War I, and settled in Palestine in 1921, working as a road labourer and simultaneously publishing poems and literary articles. In 1925, he went to Paris to study the humanities. He has been literary Editor of Davar, Ha-aretz, *and later of* Al Hamishmar. *He has also edited the literary weeklies* Ketuvim *and* Turim *tending to modernism, and since 1951 has edited the literary quarterly* Orlogin.

His early verse shows marked influence of the then-prevailing Russian Symbolism and futurism in its rhythms, imagery and symbolical represen- tation of ideas. The contents, too, carry echoes of the Russian Revolution. The principal themes of the poems he wrote at that time are the harsh struggles of the Palestine pioneers, their arduous, monotonous toil, their loneliness and longing for the homes they left, set against their joy of crea- tion, and the ennobling sorrows of self-sacrifice.

Shlonsky's work with its wealth of metaphor, imagery, associations and new rhythms is thought to have created a new Hebrew poetic language. He is an undisputed master of language. His poetry shows keen sensi- tivity to social problems, to man's place in the universe, to his loneliness amidst the false glitter and putrefaction of the big city, and his yearning to merge again with rejuvenating nature. Most of his poems strike an individ- ual lyrical note, charged with a joie de vivre *undimmed by a hidden vein of pessimism. Frequently, there is an escape back to the world of childhood and its pure dreams, which have been shattered by reality.*

Collections of his poems have been published in numerous volumes, notably: Devay *('Pain'),* Ba-Galgal *('In the Cycle'),* Le-Abba—Ima *('To Father—Mother'),* Be-Eleh ha-Yamim *('Nowadays'),* Avney Tohu

('Stones of Chaos'), Shirey ha-Mapolet veha-Piyus ('Poems of Cataclysm and Conciliation'), Shirey ha-Yamim ('Songs of the Days'), Al Milet ('Inlaid with Jewels'), Avney Gevil ('Unhewn Stones'). His collected poems were published in two large volumes.

Some of his literary and art reviews and studies of language have been published in the collection Yalkut Eshel.

Shlonsky is regarded as one of the finest translators in modern Hebrew literature and has rendered classics from several languages into Hebrew, among them works by Shakespeare, Molière, Pushkin, Block, Brecht, Gogol, Rolland, De Coster, Gorki, Makarenko, Sologub, Simonov, Kropotkin, Trotsky and Babel.

Dress Me Mother

Dress me, mother dear, in a striped shirt of splendour
And at the break of dawn
Lead me to work.

My land is wrapped in light as in a prayer-shawl.
Houses stand forth like frontlets.
The roads we paved stretched out
Like philacter-thongs.

A graceful city offers a prayer to its Creator,
And among those who created it
You can count your son Avraham,
Poet-saviour in Israel.

At dusk Father will return from his toil
And murmur a blissful prayer:
Avraham my dearest son,
All skin and bone and sinew,
Halleluiah!

Dress me, mother dear, in a striped shirt of splendour
And at the break of dawn
Lead me to work.

Translated by Abraham Birman

Many Many A Time

Many many a time
The bells will yet chime
In the gloaming
Of bluish lands.

Many a golden shoe
We shall wear out, roaming
In the sands.

Many a tear
We shall shed
(We who have loved so well)
To the chiming of the bells.

Translated by Abraham Birman

A Hotel Room

The room here is right-angled, as in all hotels,
But very long
And not too high
And narrow.
Here in the gloom you manage all-too-well
To whisper 'God' in adolescent terror.

To press a torrid brow against a window-pane
(The eye, you know, can hear at such an hour),
And like a hound whose master has been slain,
Frustrated silence in the darkness howls.

At such an hour, by inspiration's chord,
A perfect square of loftiness is twisted,
And my attentive eyes an alien town behold
Unfolding like a train's nocturnal vista.

Translated by Abraham Birman

At the End of the Nights

[I]

Everything goes into hiding yet dazzles.
Everything screams 'I exist not!' yet stays.
Everything falters, too baffled to frazzle
Your X-raying gaze.

Is that why we quailed, sorely tempted to run
Away from the good and succumb to the wicked?
If only we managed, O Tangible One,
To take our eyes off the trigger!

But you, too, are weary of playing acquitter
And once more ensnare us, hellbound.
And once more a steely-eyed boa-constrictor
Is holding us riveted, spellbound.

[II]

To you and to you, to the end of the nights,
To the margin of days, never dead though extinguished;
Where, turgid as dunes, all the crimes of mankind
Swell up unredressed, unrelinquished.

Look at a man's hand: it's crying out.
Look at his soul: it's afraid to borrow.
Condone his embarrassment, honour his doubts,
The tortuous grin that betrays his horror.

Hosanna, Hosanna, yet no succour comes!
If you have forgotten to grasp and forbear,
Then spare us your watchfulness' bonus,
Have mercy upon us
And let us repair.

Translated by Abraham Birman

Prayer

Forgive me, you whom we call by a name,
Revealed one whose pure shining fills my eye.
I am not guilty, I am not to blame
That in our speech words slur and fall awry.

Ours is a speech we've often tried to test
Upon your beasts: they didn't understand.
Perhaps our cradle was not in the waste,
And the first hand was not a father's hand.

For when at first the bright horns of red day
Clashed on the night's eternal forehead, my
Primeval father knew the proper way
To bellow answer to the ram's great cry.

And the rain spoke to grass, the lamb heard thunder,
And all heard Cain and Abel. As for us,
What more are we to do? We sit and wonder,
Sending our words out into emptiness.

Forgive me, you whom we call by a name,
Forgive these words, this tongue confusion twists.
I am not guilty, I am not to blame.
Teach me to bellow like you with your beasts.

Translated by Dom Moraes

Covet Not

Wheat in the wind. Fragrance. Thorn.
Dark night. Dark night and seed.
Release me and forgive, Forgiver,
the evil of our need.

We coveted walking, walking, walking.
You command us: "Stand still!"
Rebellion is distress, captivity affliction.
"Covet not!" be Your stern will.

Because we have drawn near
the boundaries of fright,
bid us "Here! No further!" Bid us: "Rest!"
Seed in the meadow. Wheat in the wind.
And night.
Dark night and silence.

Translated by Robert Friend

Hail

When treetops flutter on a stormy night
One seems to hear a distant rumbling sound:
Stars falling prostrate on the ground
As ripe fruit fall down when you shake a tree.

And then
When even roots' complacence is disturbed
They may console themselves, safe in the clods,
And say,
"How wise indeed we were to hide so deep."

But what will all those God's birds do
When hailstones pelt them in the open sky?

Translated by Abraham Birman

Mr. X Speaks of His Neighbourhood

I live in a house that is 5 floors high.
The windows are yawning at what stands opposite
Like faces that look into mirrors.

In my city there are 70 bus routes,
Packed to choking and full of the stench of bodies.
They travel
And travel
And travel deep into the heart of the city:
Almost as if one couldn't be killed by boredom
Right here in my neighbourhood.

It's very small, my neighbourhood.
Still, it has its births and its deaths,
And all the things that happen in between
In all the cities there are—
Even brilliant children spinning a hoop
And 3 cinemas.
If I didn't find the boredom in my own home so adequate
I would visit one of the cinemas.

I live in a house that is 5 floors high.
The woman who jumped from the window opposite
Found 3 were adequate.

Translated by Dom Moraes

Envy

I do not envy you your stellar riches
In alienated distances,
O Turning Sword of Solitude.

I'd rather have this forest
Where treetops touch befriendingly
And trunks are worlds apart.

The wind, caressing oaks and bushes
As if they both were new-born babes,
Will now play havoc with my hair until
Some birds mistake it for a tree and seek
To build a nest there for their fledgelings.
And God, so merciful and kind,
Tired of the ruthless grandeur,
Will turn His eyes from His abysmal heavens
And see that my abode is good.

But oh, the feller, Father, oh, the headsman—
I hear his footsteps,
I see his swinging arms
And envy then the quietude of stars.

Translated by Abraham Birman

Sabbath Stars

The Sabbath stars have climbed high, more peaceful than you
Who are sad today.
Your sadness is almost blasphemy—
Blowing out the careful candles Mother lit.

You, you who swore yourself into silence,
The essence of human speech,
Like honey, the privilege of a thousand roses,
Like a landscape where there is a pact of peace
Between wood and mountain and brook, to live as one,
Waging no wars, and yet to live alone—

Flow with your times and the children of your times,
Flow to your end as the river flows
To a known sea with a shore—

Where from wet sand the children knead new loaves,
And a seashell, knowing no words,
Still sighs in your ear the secret
Of low tide and high.

The Sabbath stars have climbed high, more peaceful than you.

Translated by Dom Moraes

YOCHEVED BAT-MIRIAM

1901—

*Poetess. Born in White Russia, she received a traditional Jewish upbringing,
attended university in Odessa and Moscow, and settled in Palestine in 1928.*

Her early poetry, published in the collection Me-Rahok *('From Afar'),
is lyrically romantic, concerned with love and with yearning for the atmos-
phere of sanctity pervading her father's house, which has been left behind.
Her later verse, published in the collection* Reayon *('Interview'), shows
the marked influence exerted by the Russian Symbolists; rich in imagery,
it tends to obscurity. The poems collected in* Demuyot Me-Ofek *('Images
from the Horizon') are forceful and compact, conjuring up memories of
the distant world the writer has left behind her. Her Palestine poems view
the present from the aspect of eternity.*

Other collections of poems are: Eretz Israel *('The Land of Israel'),*
Mi-Shirey Russia *('Songs of Russia'),* Shirim La-Ghetto *('Ghetto Verse'),
and* Shirim, *a choice selection.*

A Bird with the Slenderest Legs

A bird with the slenderest legs
And feathers so soft and so fine,
Embroidered in colours, in gold,
Dearest present of mine.

Its wings—like an evening in forests,
Its eyes—the bluest of green,
It gazed at unseen skies of radiance
Like a prisoner in a far away sheen.

Then dull heavy rumblings arose
With the scent of great waters' doom
And the whispering of wonderful plants
Came towering and sharp to my room.

And my heart beat loudly and burrowed
A yearning long long refused,
Like the memory of a far distant homeland,
Moaning, petulant, confused.
And the walls of my room stood erect,
Each one alone with no ceiling,
And I raised to the stars like a lamp
My face that was shining and reeling.

Translated by Richard Flantz

I am Five Foot Tall

I am five foot tall.
It is five foot as well,
The plot of land set aside
For my last sleep of all.

Like a window wide to the wind
Of height and distances—
Each day that rises seems
Hung over an abyss.

It sobs, sobs in my palm
As a last farewell on the way—
Each hand that is stretched to greet,
And, bewildered, pulls away.

And, bewildered, each neck cranes,
Like a child whose mother did
Not soothe its tears away,
Who, helpless, in dumbness hid.

How to shut my ears to their cry?
How avert my eyes, when there is
A brightness on every brow,
A light from beyond all this?

Like the going of a tearful man
Each step falters, and almost falls.
Pardon is shed from my eyes.
Ask pardon from all for all.

Translated by Dom Moraes

They Sit

They sit, still they sit, old ancient women
On the stoop of the slumbering synagogue,
As on a fainting shore between fact and fantasy,
Staring unstirring in still setting fog.

They sit bent and huddled, silent and sad
In a single radiance that has passed on and died,
As though spun out and spun, they sail on and on
With the last secret ray of light.

Prayer books open towards leaning horizons
Inclined in desire to see and divine
The splendours of a world that dreams of itself
Among spaces between letters and signs.

Stillness and the calm of moments that flow,
Flowing free to that other shore,
Wandering and wondering, lucid and rolling,
Bits of an eternity that gleams evermore.

Until the first days and last days unite
In a single secret unsolved and sealed.
Till from age-wrinkled pages there arise, branching out,
Trees of an Eden unknown and concealed.

Their shade lying over the dying of skies,
Of animals and earth and the sward,
Where a single sun shines, yellow, alone,
Like the initial of the name of the Lord.

They sit, still they sit, old ancient women
On the stoop of the slumbering synagogue,
As on a fainting shore between fact and fantasy,
Staring unstirring in still setting fog.

Translated by Richard Flantz

If He Returns

If he returns—he'll lift me into his car
That flies up blazing and high,
And he'll bring me his warm smiling breadth
And the calm blue distance in his eye

From sights that were lost in the flames,
That paced through the storm's dreadful slings
Among pieces of serpents and stones,
And animals, faces and wings—

Not a word will I be able to say,
Not a thing will I be able to show
Of his height that keeps rising higher,
Of his good and gentle glow,

My glance will ripen like bread,
My face will rise like a fruit.
For he's brought me,
He's brought me to tears,
In a daily holiness to brood.

I shall break my crust into two
And wait on my stoop, hand on knee,
They will come:
The wanderer, the blue—
To drink my water with me.

Translated by Richard Flantz

] 333 [

Parting

And dawn shall trail after me to the shore,
Like a child, to play with shells:
Singing like a hope, shining like a tear,
Silent, the echo of what will befall.

On chill and sun he will inscribe his height
In a tall wide script: he shall not claim
Any remembrance of my form in flight,
My name, my humble other name.

My name which went singing for happiness,
For many griefs, and times I went astray.
With and above it, like a faltering promise
Stepped my great day.

A bit of it—like a scent, an echo—
I contained in the blue vase,
In the Chinese drawing made long ago.
Longing for its butterfly, its stalk of grass.

And a few books, not many, which looked out
At their moon leaving the river, on its way.
It taught a warm and festive solitude
And the sharp lustre of the faraway.

When the parting suddenly flings wide forever
The unknown distance, in a little while,
I'll remember everything by name, by the quiver
Of their wise and bashful smile.

I shall put my dead face on with a silence free
Of joy and of pain evermore,
And dawn will trail like a child after me
To play with shells on the shore.

Translated by Dom Moraes

Come Out Here

Come out here, where there's lightning and rain
And that freedom which, combining,
Light up in the heart of bushes and grass
Their burnt vegetation of rebellious-pining.

Come out here suddenly hearing,
Your own loneliness calling near at hand.
The voice, like an echo torn from a step,
The voice like a ransom to the borderland.

Your body sails off from shoulder height,
Loneliness grows like winging bands.
Live. Live!—
   Wings flap in flight.
Live. Live!
   No-voice commands.

Translated by Richard Flantz

Flame, Compressed Heat

Flame, compressed heat, smell of water and sand,
Of man's body earthward reaching.
Heavens, heavens smoking on the path,
Weary of not approaching.

Get up and cross! Even if you stand,
The routine most certainly known
Must estrange you with dark secret marvels
Like the purpose sought always alone.

And you will be feast-day and temple,
The direction, the misery—the guest
Time. His memory crystallized in changes,
The despair of their febrile behest.

Till you sink to the dust.
From silence and lonely dearth
Like a spring from mountains of frost
God will yearn to rake up the earth
Of the road where your shadow crossed.

Translated by Richard Flantz

LEVI BEN-AMITAI

1901—

Poet. Born in Lachowitz, White Russia, he settled in Palestine in 1920 and worked as a road and building labourer. In 1925, he joined kibbutz Deganya Bet, worked on the land and in 1939 became a teacher there.

His verse, popular in nature, is devoted to the humble tiller of the soil, the Jewish farmer in his homeland. It exalts all creative work, particularly that of the farmer, which the poet places on a level with the duties performed by the Priests and Levites in the Temple. The poet identifies himself with the pure simple lives of the ancient Essenes, whose modern counterparts are the kibbutz members.

His published collections of poems are: Ha-Shibolim Penima, Leilot Ba-matzor *('Nights under Siege'),* Ba-kevutza *('In the Kevutza'),* Sadot Sheba-Emek *('The Fields of the Valley'),* Oholiva *('The temple'),* Mid-bar Matana *('From the Desert, a Gift'), and* Shirim Al ha-Isim *('Poems on the Essenes').*

In the Kibbutz

Each day I rake the piles of dung that fall
To earth beneath the legs of drowsing cows,
Or knead some mortar, mending breaches in the wall,
Or walk behind the horses in the furrows.

Humble is my life in this Thy world of light,
A hewer of wood, I, a bearer of water,
A man without a name, a Gibeonite:
Eternal slave in Jerusalem's holy quarter.

When twilight comes I wash my hands and face,
Put on myself a shirt of clean white cloth,
And in the company of priests I take my place,
And on the table find my bread and broth.

Seated with levites to the humblest of suppers,
I raised up my voice in a hymn to Thy praise:
Blessed art Thou for the good dung that succours,
For the small crust of bread and the fervour of prayer.

Translated by Richard Flantz

The Fields of Jezreel

The fields of the Valley
Greet me this evening
With the scent of manure
And the odour of hay.
Tonight, in the valley,
A hymn I am singing,
For I have found grace here,
And am grateful and gay.

For I have returned
To your dales and your furrows—
From the deathbed of sorrows,
From the grief for my dead;
By the toil of my hands
This blessing I'm granted:
To drink of your waters
And to eat of your bread.

Oh come now and reap me
With the crop that you're gathering—
Like a ripe heavy corn-ear,
Upon harvest day;
Tonight, to the Valley,
A hymn I am singing,
For I have found grace here,
And am grateful and gay.

Translated by Richard Flantz

Sabbath in the Kibbutz

Mother Sabbath lays white cloths upon the tables
And lights the candles with an unseen hand—
She has gathered her sons from their six days of labour
To a family meal.

Light falls on the tables, shadows lurk round walls —
There is shadow in wrinkles, light on sunburnt arms;
And shirts gleam white around shoulders and necks,
Like prayer-shawls.

The warm dark night has wrapped the valley to the universe,
The sea of Galilee breathes in ripples of soft waves,
The song of night is in the fields and the cricket saws
For dancing butterflies.

What is this ancient image rising? A tribe of shepherds?
A family sacrifice? A public feast?
Why does the heart thrill to the memory of Essenes
And Jordan-dwellers of old?

There are eyes here have delved into unstudied futures,
And eyes that have filled with trembling or joy—
And someone furtively feels sorrow in her soul—
And her tear heals...

Light is sown on the table. It rises and grows:
As eyes meet eyes, new sparks are born.
The shadows have fled from the wall, where pass the white hands
Of unseen Mother Sabbath.

] 343 [

Mother Sabbath! Do you hear the pounding of hearts
And the silence of lips this night on the Jordan?
They thirst for prayer. Spread your hands over this bread
And bless them.

Bless the faithful, the sowers of light in the fields of man—
And put the world's joy into hearts longing for brotherhood.
More will yet come, all to sit together like brothers
At the Sabbath of rest...

Translated by Richard Flantz

HAIM LENSKI

1905—?

Poet. Born of a poor family in Slonim, White Russia, he went from Poland to Russia in 1924. He sent his Hebrew poems to Palestine, where they were published in various literary journals. In 1935, he was sentenced to five years' imprisonment in a Siberian labour camp, but managed to get his poems sent to Palestine during this period.

No details are known of his eventual fate. A book of his poems, written in 1940-41, was received in Israel in 1957.

Lita ('Lithuania'), his major poetic work, depicts childhood scenes. Other poems describe the Siberian landscape, express the gloom of imprisonment, show admiration for the Hebrew language and reflect on man's struggles and longings.

His collected verse has been published under the titles Ha-Anaf ha-Gadua *('The Hewn-off Branch') and* Me-Ever la-Nahar ha-Letti *('Beyond the Lett River').*

How Soft, How Warm the Evening

How soft, how warm the evening!
The touch of the wind, how light!
A sickle moon is lifted
On a flood of rays, rose-bright.

With his starry eye peers Saturn.
What can he discern?
Somewhere a bird is mourning:
No yesterdays return.

Translated by Robert Friend

Wormwood has Enchanted Me

Wormwood has enchanted me completely,
With bitterness of juices sharply smelling.
For wormwood's sake and only for its sake,
I wander, Cain, a man without a dwelling;
A shoot of wandering, by the east-wind beaten,
And for no sin, stoned by the sharp-edged hail.
Its hair of greenish-white is more compelling,
Is dearer to me than the red of roses,
Or even your lips' red, O Beauty's daughter.
No, do not mock me with your laughter.
I'm not a saint. I'm not an anchorite—
Wormwood has enchanted me completely.

Translated by Robert Friend

Day Turns to Evening

Day turns to evening on the lake.
The fish descend to sleep and the wave hushes.
Birds cease their chatter in the brake.
How melancholy are the rustling rushes!

The echo of what voice complains?
The echo of whose voice where the reeds sway?
The shore is desolate. No foot has trod these plains
Since the world's first day.

Of longings that have found no words,
Of days whose sun set long ago,
Of the migrations of the birds—
The rushes whisper to the lake below.

Translated by Robert Friend

Incredible Splendour...

Incredible splendour—ethereal, delicate!
What transparency!
With one slight breath drawn from the deep breast,
The pattern that we know ceases to be.

Uprooted, everything is flying.
No wonder that a leaf—a leaf?—a tree is soaring.
There is no miracle, and not one thing is hidden.
Everything's revealed. The tree, the whole tree's soaring.

You raise your voice—no echo; you bend your head—no shadow.
You are lighter than the webs of late September.
Matter shakes off the burden of its weight
As riffling a book's pages frees it of its words.

Translated by Robert Friend

Lightly a Slight Shadow

Lightly a slight shadow floats on the March snows.
Look! a starling is making its swift flight.
The horizon is pierced by its bill. A chick
from the crack of eggshell thinness pecks its way.

Another day! Another day!
The stream bursts through its carapace of ice,
and the first thunder
shatters the silence of fields.
To their old nests birds return with a song.
My land, I shall see thee, I will see thee yet.

Translated by Robert Friend

Fresh is the Air

Fresh is the air when the storm is spent
And cloud after cloud has vanished into space.
A silence drenched with forest scent
Floats, purged of the dross of time and place.

Though darkness' shadow dims the whole world yet,
Already in the sky a patch of azure smiles.
The horizon slopes are split
By bursts of a rain that dwindles down the miles.

Translated by Robert Friend

The Moon's Brightness

The moon's brightness turns a freezing blue;
She trembles as if taken by a fever.
An hour will pass, a second, or a third—
And the storm will break forth in anger.

Over land and island, over the sea
Her majesty the storm will soon be sweeping.
Armed with the lightning, to the beat of the thunder's drum,
Cloud legions will come streaming.

Our generation's ruled by the house of Mars,
And the hand of fate cannot be stayed, my brother.
I know this well, since drunk with insanity's wine,
We kill each other.

And yet the storm will end, a rain will fall,
A quiet meadow wind stir into being,
And over a dead tree trunk, a waking bluebell
With tongue of dew will carol in the morning.

Translated by Robert Friend

There Broke into My Cell

There broke into my cell last night
A whistle from the train of winds.
Though I was half asleep, feet leaped ahead.
"Forward, while strength remains!"

Forward! And in a flash I stood
Upon a train step, at a door.
Nobody asked, "Where from?" Nor I,
"Where are you headed for?"

Darkness flowed like streams of tar
Round about my window pane
As shawls of snow from the north pole waved
Good-bye to the departing train.

South to the homeland! But who had changed
The window to a drum and hit it?
A finger at the judas-window rapped:
"Hiding beneath the covers not permitted."

Translated by Robert Friend

SHIN SHALOM

1905—

Poet. Born in Galicia, the son of the Hassidic Rebbe of Drohobycz, he lived in Vienna (1914-22) and then in Palestine. He attended the Jerusalem Teachers' Training College, taught, and studied philosophy at German universities.

Much of his poetry strikes a mystical religious note, charged with symbols and probing into the hidden recesses of the esoteric and its barely-discerned flitting shadows. His poems strive to fathom the depths of the soul of man, the soul of the nation, the soul of the world, so as to learn the secret and reason for their existence. They are pervaded with pessimism regarding the fate of man, for whom every kindled torch is the stake. From behind this decadent pessimism there emerges a dream of a new reality, where a positive factor unites man's world.

His Biblical poems, filled with a moral element, express optimistic faith in the ultimate victory of the upright. In his love poems he conceives love as a divine force contending with death. His autobiographical poem On Ben Peleh depicts his own striving for what is great and sacred. He has also written topical verse, reacting sharply to contemporary social and political events.

His poetic works have been collected and published under the titles: Be-Lev Olam ('In the Heart of the World'), Mi? ('Who?') Panim el Panim ('Face to Face'), Yerushalayim Tira Nama ('Jerusalem, Slumbering City'), Sefer ha-Shirim veha-Sonnetot ('Book of Poems and Sonnets'), Shabbat ha-Olam ('Sabbath of the World'), Ilan ba Ruah ('A Tree in the Wind'), Hayinu ke-Holmim ('We were as Dreamers'), Mi-Toch ha-Lehavot ('From Amidst the Flames'), Olam ba-Ruah ('Wind-tossed World').

Prose poems and drama: Ha-Yad ha-Sheniya ('The Other Hand'), Yoman ba-Galil ('Galilee Diary'), Ha-Ner lo Kava ('The Light was not Extinguished'), Adama u-Shemey Shamayim ('Earth and Highest Hevean'), Be-Metah Gavoah ('High Tension'), Yeriot al Kibbutz ('Kibbutz under Fire').

He has also translated Shakespeare's sonnets into Hebrew.

Shofarot*

In grandfather's house, Atonement Day drew near.
The sacred trumpet blew so loud, so much,
The pregnant women would come at dusk to hear,
And smooth my bedclothes with an absent touch.

Their eyes knew secrets, brimming with a tear
As they smoothed down my sheet. I did not see:
What has this gentle hand that draws so near
To do with sorrow none can remedy?

An amulet lay on my breast: they'd bend
To press soft lips there, shuddering painfully.
And then I prayed that this would never end,
For sweet and soft their lips were, touching me.

So smooth their cheeks were, drawn across my cheek,
I wanted more; my mouth was moved to ask.
But all the sacred trumpets would suddenly speak
And every face would turn to a white mask.

Translated by Dom Moraes

*Shofarot—rams' horns blown on the Day of Atonement.

When a Man Dies

When a man dies in the Valley of Jezreel,
the grain stalks hush.
A holy of holies is the Valley of Jezreel,
no place for mourning.

When night descends on the Valley of Jezreel,
the stars tremble,
candles in the Valley of Jezreel
for those no *Kaddish* remembers.

Translated by Robert Friend

Black Sheep

Upon the slope, the black sheep suddenly
looked up at me,
and then went on, eyes glassy-bright
to sink into the night...

I said: Perhaps I went wrong at a turning.
Or do they know
who— as I climbed, eyes yearning—
pushed me below?

I said, I'll follow them until I see
the meaning of this mystery:
why mountain brothers did not know a brother,
nor that his gods are other.

I've hurled away my compass and my chart,
my watch as well.
You are my brothers now—you, singing flute,
clapper that strikes the bell.

The night is heavy and the night appals,
the rain falls.
Upon the slope, the black sheep suddenly
looked up at me...

Translated by Robert Friend

Not All is So Simple

Not all is so simple in the courtyards of town.
From high and low storeys the windows stare down.
On bareness of pavement, on faded brick wall,
each hour is inscribed, each hour with its scrawl.

Not all is so simple in a mirror's deep glance;
there is something to read in a bookcase's stance.
A curtain though heavy, a bed, iron-wrought,
sink under the burden, the weight of a thought.

In the dark of the houses, how silent are they—
the creatures descending, the first light of day,
ascending at evening the dark of the stairs,
then closing their doors. For these are my prayers.

Translated by Robert Friend

Wonders

Wonders drink, my heart. My heart, imbibe the wonder.
What day to day will bring, no night will rift asunder.
Strip and dive into ebullient precision:
Every touch an image, every sight a vision.

Choose the path, my heart. My heart, select the trail
Where man will reign supreme, where dancing will prevail.
Wherever you wander, wherever you rest
The secret will abide with you, the wind will be your guest.

Sing a song, my heart. My heart, sing a song
To endless light, to bliss immeasurably long.
Fill your cup and drink to pleasure and to sadness.
Welcome life with joy and welcome death with gladness.

Translated by Abraham Birman

Ars Poetica

You came to me with Nietzsche and his Superman's horsewhip,
You came to me with Baudelaire and his *Fleurs du Mal*.
You came to me with Carlyle and his hero-worship,
You came to me with Rimbaud, that terrible "Shakespeare's Child".
You came and you thrust my song into my hand like a dagger,
But I hurled it down at the feet of my brother, the beggar.

But I have seen a hungry baby pule and writhe,
And I heard a lonely woman utter a shout in alarm.
To a pain named Israel I am paying a regular tithe,
And I am the one to embrace a toil-stained arm.
But I lit up my life to illumine a desolate hovel,
And now, with a censer of ashes, in front of your temple I grovel.

And now I shall cling to my song like a derelict anchor,
And now my lines like the iron of smiths I shall forge.
Because I'm defeated you smile in contempt at my rancour,
But proudly I gaze at the smoke of the smouldering torch.
Now I know—empty-handed I went but triumphant return.
You brought me the image of Man and I gave it a love none can
   spurn.

Translated by Abraham Birman

Michelangelo to the Finger of God

Open a cleft in the marble block
To channel my blood's lively course.
Give me strength from the heart of the rock
To quarry my own resource.
Grant me a desperate need
To fashion, to knead.

Help me to flutter and hover
Along with my heaviest kit.
Give me the presence of mind to recover
My foundering wits.
Endow me with tone and nuance
That save from mischance.

Chastise me to hunger, to thirst,
From dungeons to crave for the light,
To strive though my lot be reversed
In the valley of fright,
To carve on ephemeral bark
Love's eternal mark.

Translated by Abraham Birman

The Dance of the Torches

*They say that on every Simkhat
Bet Ha'shoeva (Libation Festival),
Rabban Shimon Ben Gamliel used
to juggle eight torches in the
air, throwing one lighted torch
and catching another, and they
never touched.*
                        (Sukkah 53.)

Forward, honest torch; backward, fulsome torch;
  onward, sober torch; glory is a torch.
Justice is a torch; kindness is a torch;
  nothingness a torch; everything a torch.
Throw the shackled one; catch the tackled one;
  summon glow and fun to the blazing pyre;
Crookedness is fair; circle is a square;
  sacrilege a snare; boulders—seas of fire.
Volatile and deep; diving bold and steep;
  lucid and opaque; manacled and free.
Sluggish and alert; dashing and inert;
  with discretion girt to control the spree.

Up goes the glance
Down goes the dance.
Thrill with mildness blended,
Swing by sloth amended.
If one torch should drop
The whole dance will flop.

Hearts with pride will swell; hosts of Israel;
  flocks of Miriam's Well, with my heartblood watered.

Stigma, stain and stitch; arrows' flight and swish;
  tone and sound and pitch all around me quartered.
Loads of water tote for the lambs and goats;
  soon my burning throat rabid flames will swallow.
Clapping hand to hand; wielding magic wands;
  tears in silent lands with a star to follow.
Worlds to pieces fall; light disperses all;
  sparks demurely call at eternal gates.
Countless battles won; countless flickers gone;
  only Love is one, but the torches—eight!

Translated by Abraham Birman

Incense

Night of sleeplessness,
night of no sleep.
I strap my knapsack on, containing nothing,
and go to tour a town that has no name.

A man is not a man,
a tower is not a tower,
but feels the height as if it pressed upon its spire;
but I from its one window discover all the world.

There I shall stand,
there, watching on high,
heart wholly still, body a whispering brand,
like a cloud of incense climbing towards the sky.

Translated by Robert Friend

The Scapegoat

On the Day of Atonement
The High Priest died,
So the Prefect took his place.
He drew the lots,
Slaughtered his bullock
And sprinkled its blood.
Then they brought him
The sacrificial goat
And he received its blood in a basin.
He went into the Holy of Holies
And took up his stance
But did not prolong his prayer
Lest the people of Israel take fright,
For the Temple was filled with smoke
And the sun was about to set.

Then he approached the Scapegoat
And laid his hands upon it
And made confession:
"O God, Thy people,
The House of Israel
Have committed iniquity,
Transgressed and sinned before thee.
O God, forgive—"

And they delivered the Scapegoat
To the emissary who was scheduled
To lead it away,

And they made a causeway for it
Because of the Chaldeans
Who used to pull its hair
Crying, "Bear our sins and be gone,
Bear and be gone..."
And some of the notables of Jerusalem
Went with him as far as the first booth
Erected for this purpose.
There were ten booths
From Jerusalem to the ravine,
A distance of ninety *ris*
(A *ris* measured seven and a half to the mile).
At every booth they said to him,
"Here is food,
Here is water"
To break him in
And keep him happy.

When they came to the last booth
(For none went with him to the ravine
But all stood aloof
And watched his doings)
Night had covered everything,
The tongue of flame had grown dim
And the emissary's heart beat fast
As they went along.

In silence they trudged together,
Never turning to look behind them,
And fear marched ahead
Like the fear of the Ineffable Name.
All of a sudden, as if

By common consent
The emissary began to walk on all-fours
And the scapegoat at his side
Began to walk erect, like
A human being...
He twirled his bushy beard,
Blinked his greenish eyes
And his teeth shone in the darkness
Like a doorway to a wanton world.
Bending down he whispered to the man
Who did not know how, all of a sudden,
He understood the goat's language:
"The high and mighty are standing
In the ornate court of the Temple,
Waiting for the sign that the scapegoat
Has atoned for their sins.
It shall not be!
Today our fates are reversed:
I will be the emissary
And you shall be the scapegoat.

"Today I am taking you, stranger,
From your brethren's stockades of servitude,
From the moments' fortified mansion
To Azazel, the State of Insurgence,
To be thrown into the abyss of flame,
Every limb a separate auricle,
A rolling zodiac of life.

"Today I am taking you, stranger,
From your brethren's stockade of servitude,
From domain of shrine and temple,

From the realm of the binding flesh,
To be the blood that shrieks at night,
A stellular wound on every stone,
Gaping at horror and wonder,
Exposed to the onslaught of the storm..."

Hardly had the scapegoat spoken
When folly possessed him
And he skipped and hopped
Running his eyes to and fro,
Green eyes of flame,
Horns shining in the darkness,
Butting the man.
And the emissary tripped and fell.

The sound of his breaking bones
Was heard throughout the night,
And all that time
The green eyes of the scapegoat
Burned like live coals.

And the people languished on and on,
The High Priest's prayer was held up,
And a stifled rumour persisted:
"The emissary failed to return."

Translated by Abraham Birman

AVRAHAM BROIDES

1907—

Poet. Born in Vilna, he came to Palestine in 1923 and worked as a road and factory labourer. He is one of the founders of the Ha-noar Ha-oved (Working Youth) movement, and has been secretary of the Hebrew Writers' Association for the past thirty-seven years.

His poems have a social character, often devoted to the simple, humble man. His early work is marked by such themes as the Palestinian pioneers, the wonder of the homeland that is being rebuilt, love, nature, home and family as well as topical events. His later work is contemplative; it expresses a yearning for purification of spirit—the world of purity of the ancient Essenes—set in the awe-inspiring landscapes of Safed and Ein Gedi.

His published collections of poems are: Ba-telem ('In the furrow'), Eshnav ('Skylight'), Mi-bayit ('From Home)', Emunim ('Fidelity'), Kol ('A Voice'), La'ad ('Forever'), Ba-tzar ('In Adversity'), Magen Va-Shir ('Shield and Song'), Bekum Israel ('When Israel Arose'), Mi-Adam le-Adam ('From Man to Man'), Shorashim ba-Sela ('Roots in the Rock'), and El-ha-Shachar ha-Ganuz ('To the Hidden Dawn').

At An Orphaned Hour

Even all that is common, transparent and simple
Wears the shade of a dark hidden wonder.
The strings of weeping and joy start to tremble,
Touched by blind hands of a conjurer.

Never will you know the secret, the whisper,
Between speechless house-walls of chalk.
There are crannies that hide the snake and the sorcerer,
And the pigeon that turns to a hawk.

And so, turbulent, with terrified tremor,
Among walls and tenants I'll run.
And at an orphaned hour I shall plead in a murmur:
"Forgive me, my wife and my son..."

Translated by Richard Flantz

On the Mount of Essenes

I have vowed unspeakable vows,
I have learned the steep way of silence.
To concealed crypts of secret signs
My path has parted,
Gaining distance.

The desert has gathered me up!
The spirit of God fills its vastness, hiding in its fortresses.
The shadow of a lone bird covered my head
In a desolate mountain crevice.
I have had enough of ostentation, of the city of futility,
The salvation of the hasty.

My way is to the sect of secret ones.
I have fumbled on curves of ravines and ladders.
I have befriended the hard rock and its crags.
To my bones I have denied the taste of an artful hour.
I have suffered remorse, fever and agony:
Peeled from the trappings of my vanity
That from within myself I might fly to the heights.

To stream on in that secret exaltation!
There is no salvation nor freedom in the essence of priests—
And happiness dwells not on the altars of ceremony...

Closeness to the Almighty
Is in the waves of the voids, in the closed caves of cliffs,
Since before the ages of wilderness

In unstudied stillness,
Crying to him.

His sources will rain for the thirsty in spirit,
For the pure and devoted few;
The estate of his goodness is to the humble,
For his followers—manna and dew.

Translated by Richard Flantz

My Soul

I have made journeys to my soul
But have not arrived at its mysteries.
My soul in invisible cycles
Dispels
Illusions of certainty
And the bliss of serenity.
Never can man grasp his soul
As it presses and twists
In his ribs.

My soul was to me
Like a skipping bird on a bough—
Heavier than bleak rock is it now.

Translated by Richard Flantz

SHIMSHON MELZER

1909—

Poet. Born in Poland in 1909, he attended a Teachers' Seminary there and settled in Palestine in 1933, where he became a member of the editorial board of the daily newspaper 'Davar' and later of the publishing-house 'Am Oved', as well as editor of various journals.

His poems deal primarily with hassidic and folkloristic themes, and he has a fondness for presenting legendary motifs in ballad form. He has also composed delicate lyrics, love-songs, and nature-poems. His works include Be-Shiva Meitarim *('On Seven Strings' 1938),* Meir Ha-Klizmar Na'asa Kommisar *('Meir the Bandsman Becomes a Commissar' 1940),* Lilach *and* Asara Shearim *('Ten Gates' 1943),* Alef 1945, Sefer Ha-Shirot veha-Baladot *('Book of Songs and Ballads' 1951), and* Or Zerua *('Light is Sown' 1959).*

He has translated widely from Yiddish, Polish, and German and received the Tschernikhovsky Prize for his translation of the works of Peretz.

Rabbi Zusha's Dance

And the rabbi, Rabbi Zusha with his brother Rabbi Melekh
Got up one fine morning, ere the sun had lifted high its crown,
Purified themselves, put on the clothing of a pauper *helekh*,*
Threw their knapsacks on their shoulders and departed from the town.

For the rabbi Elimelech and his brother Rabbi Zusha
Could not bide domestic pleasures and enjoy their easy fruit.
"Wake up, Melekh *dushe,* wake up!" "Hurry, Zusha *sertse,* hurry!"
And they set out on their journey on a self-imposed *Galút*.

And they set out in the morning and they went through field and forest,
And they heard the birds that blithely twittered from an unseen nest.
Cows were grazing in the meadow, lowing when their need was sorest,
Shepherds crossed themselves while eating, shepherdesses sang with
    zest.

And the overflowing song was manifoldly sweet and tender—
From below the brook emits it, from within—the joyful heart.
Everything was wrapped in glory, everything was fraught with
    splendour,
And the body melts away, the soul is ready to depart...

On the way, they know, there is an inn that gives the beggar shelter,
Food and drink, for there the landlord is an honest, pious Jew,
So his doors are open day and night to those who freeze or swelter,
And the wayfarer can rest there and his heart is gladdened, too.

*See Glossary at the end of the poem.

] 379 [

He would welcome them as Abraham had welcomed homeless
    strangers.
He would give them food and drink and shelter for the stormy night.
In the morning he would give them hard-boiled eggs, tonight's
    remainders,
For the road, until they reach another haven of respite.

Till they reach that good, secluded spot for which they have been
    yearning:
At the inn the landlord broaches wine and spirits from the wall.
Every word—a living marvel. Every look—a source of learning,
And when *tsaddiks* come they know him—right away he knows them
    all.

Till they reach that far-off haven somewhere, sometime. For the
    present
Two tired wayfarers must put up with the lowest kind of inn:
Not a scrap of food, no welcome from the landlord, not a pleasant
Spark will lighten up his countenance. His mouth—a fount of sin.

"What? A beggar here? My word, that's all I need. Upon the oven
Let him lie and warm his bones, the good-for-nothing lazy bum.
What? Another one? Together? Beggars come in twos, the loafers.
Let him lie upon the table—I have nothing else for scum."

"I shall take the table," said the rabbi Melekh to his brother.
"You should sleep upon the oven where it's warmer, Zusha love."
But Rabbi Zusha, meek and modest, said, "No, no, I'd rather
Sleep upon the table, *dushe*. You shall have the place above."

So the rabbi Elimelekh mounted on the still warm oven
And recited *Shma* and fell asleep, but Zusha was unable

To succumb to slumber. Lying in the darkness, eyes wide open,
Tossed incessantly from side to side upon the wooden table.

Thus he lay awake and tossed from side to side when lo!—a merry
Group of roisterers burst in... Commotion, whistles, shouts and song.
"Master of the winehouse, wake up! Quit your quilt and hurry, hurry!"
And the hobnailed boot beats fiercely on the flooring like a gong.

"Get a move on, landlord, rise and fetch us spirits by the gallon."
"Stronger stuff, the one that burns like fire. Make haste and bring it
    here!"
"Sit down, *koomeh,* sit down." "Move a little further up, good fellow."
Rabbi Zusha, wide awake, is listening with attentive ear.

And he hears a host of glasses filled and emptied of their liquor.
Glass to glass is lifted wildly, clashing with a gleeful note.
Lips and tongues take in the vile stuff, suck it quick and spit it quicker.
Fists are banging on the tables, cheers are bursting from the throats.

Voices soar up to the ceiling—first a solo, then a choir—
Merry voices hail a single, soulful, melancholy song.
Rapture fills the hearts and suddenly the hobnailed boots, afire,
Kick and stamp in strict accordance with the forceful, rhythmic
    throng.

Pounding on the ancient floor the hobnailed boots begin to smoulder,
Sending flames of red-hot joy from heart to heart, from man to man.
Now the arms are locked together. Now the dancers, hand-on shoulder,
Fly into a swirling tumult, kick and stamp and whirl again.

"Who dares sleep here on the table, snoring while we cheer and roister?
Wake him up and make him join the jolly, celebrating crowd!"

] 381 [

In a trice the rabbi Zusha from his wooden cot is hoisted,
And he's dancing with devotion, wheeling deftly round and round.

Great God, look down from Thy heaven and behold the sight with
    pleasure:
Rabbi Zusha sings and capers, caught up in a whirlwind dance.
On the right and on the left two *goys* are holding him together
And all three, cavorting, singing, work themselves into a trance.

Thus they sing together, yet their mouths are differently enthusing.
Goyim chant, *'Oi dana, oi danai, oi dana, oi danai'*,
But the rabbi, Rabbi Zusha, steeped into the selfsame music,
Comes up with *'Hosanna, Adonai, hosanna, Adonai'*.

Suddenly the rabbi Melekh, woken by the noisy strangers,
Sat up on the oven, eyes agape, and stared at such a sight.
And the rabbi Elimelekh heard the voice of Heaven's angels,
And his eyes, wide open now, beheld a pure, celestial light.

Then the rabbi Elimelekh knew that his dear brother Zusha
Had been dancing with the angels, singing with the seraphs' song.
And he cried, "Come, *sertse,* hurry, let me join the whirling circle,
Let me share it with you, Zusha, take me too into the throng."

But as soon as he had said this in a voice unsure, unstable,
Song and dancing vanished and the lively vision, too, was gone;
And the inn was cold and dark and in the room, upon the table,
Rabbi Zusha sighed and coughed and tossed from side to side, alone.

And the inn was cold and dark and from the oven, slowly, slowly,
Rabbi Melekh drags his feet upon the icy, stony floor.
Cold and dark—but in the rabbi Melekh's eyes still shines the holy
Light as in a meek, hushed tone he tries to whisper and implore:

"Get up, Zusha, let's change places. There, this time you take the oven
And I'll lie here. Warm your bones a little, it's a frosty night."
So the rabbi Zusha rose and got up on the little stove, and
Elimelekh, stretched upon the table, tossed from side to side.

Thus he lay and tossed from side to side when suddenly the wicket-
Gate flew open, then the portal. *They* are coming, *they* are back...
They are sitting, they are drinking, glasses fill again with liquor,
Glasses clash against each other with a merry, blissful clack.

Voices soar up to the ceiling—first a solo, then a choir—
Melancholy voices hail a single, daring, robust song.
Rapture fills the hearts and once again the hobnailed boots, afire,
Kick and stamp in strict accordance with the forceful, rhythmic song.

Pounding on the ancient floor the hobnailed boots begin to smoulder,
Sending flames of red-hot joy from heart to heart, from man to man.
Now the arms are locked together. Now the dancers, hand-on-shoulder,
Fly into a swirling tumult, kick and stamp and whirl again.

"What? The Jew's asleep once more, reposing there so limp and quiet?
Wake him up again and make him join the celebrating crowd!"
"No, no, *koomeh*, let him sleep, he's too exhausted now to riot.
There, the one upon the oven, *he* should dance and sing aloud."

Hardly had the rabbi Melekh stirred when, weightless as a feather,
Rabbi Zusha was pulled down and thrown again into the dance.
On the right and on the left two *goys* were holding him together
And all three, cavorting, singing, flew again into a trance.

Once again they chorus, yet their mouths are differently enthusing:
Goyim chant, '*Oi dana, oi danai, oi danai, oi danai*',

] 383 [

But the rabbi, Rabbi Zusha, steeped into the selfsame music,
Comes up with *'Hosanna, Adonai, hosanna, Adonai'.*

And the rabbi Elimelekh, fascinated by the strangers,
Sat up on the table, eyes agape, and marvelled at the sight.
And again the rabbi Melekh heard the voice of Heaven's angels
And his eyes, wide open now, beheld a pure, celestial light.

Then the rabbi Elimelekh knew that his dear brother Zusha
Had been dancing with the angels, joining in the seraphs' song.
And he wept and said, "This happiness was not for me. No, neither
Dance was mine, and not a single step of mine was in the throng."

But as soon as he had said this in a voice unsure, unstable,
Song and dancing vanished and the lively vision, too, was gone.
And the inn is cold and dark, and as he lies upon the table
Melekh hears his brother snore upon the oven, quite alone.

And the inn is cold and dark, and from his cot upon the table
Rabbi Melekh drags his weary feet upon the icy floor
To the oven where his brother Rabbi Zusha lies. Unable
To withold his tears he whispers in a voice unsteady, hoarse:

"Wake up, Zusha *sertse,* wake up from your slumbers, dearest
    brother—
Twice you sang and danced with angels. What good fortune, Zusha
    love!"
"Twice I danced with God's own seraphs?" "First a round and then
    another!"
And they wept together on that fateful night upon the stove.

And they wept all through the night, both Rabbi Melekh and his
  brother,
And they rose at early dawn with a much lighter heart and foot.
"Wake up, Melekh *dushe,* wake up!" "Hurry, Zusha *sertse,* hurry!"
And they set out in the morning on a self-imposed *Galút.*

Translated by Abraham Birman

GLOSSARY

Helech   (H) A wayfarer, especially a poor one.
Dushe   (R) Soul. A term of endearment.
Sertse   (R) Heart. A term of endearment. In Hassidik lore, Elimelekh was the 'soul'
                and Zusha the 'heart',
Galut   (H) Exile, wandering. Pious people often imposed this on themselves for a
                certain period of time.
Adonai   (H) God.
Goy   (H) A gentile. (Plural *goys,* also *goyim*)
Koomeh   (R) A friend.

NATAN ALTERMAN

1910—

Poet and translator. Born in Warsaw, he went to Palestine in 1925 and later studied agronomy at the University of Nancy, France.

His verse is lyrical and contemplative, rich in imagery, symbols and innovations in style and language. One of his main themes consists of a dialogue between the living and the dead, whose shades walk among the living in the hearts of those they love. Collections of his poems have been published under the titles Kochavim Bahutz ('There are Stars Outside'), Simhat Aniyim ('The Joy of the Poor'), Shirei Makot Mitsrayim ('Songs of the Plagues of Egypt') and Ir Hayonah ('City of the Dove'). His collected works were published in 1965.

A master of topical verse, he has reacted sharply and satirically to contemporary social and political events in a weekly column Ha-Tur Ha-Shevii ('Seventh Column'), later published in a two-volume collection.

He has written children's poems—Ha-Efroah ha-Asiri ('The Tenth Chick') and Sefer ha-Teva ha-Mezameret ('Book of the Singing Box)', plays—Kinneret Kinneret and Pundak ha-Ruhot ('The Inn of Ghosts') and Mishpat Pythagoras ('Pythagoras's Theorem') and has translated into Hebrew works by Racine, Shakespeare, Moliere and recently has written the lyrics for musicals such as Shlomo Hamelech VeShalmai Ha-sandlar ('King Solomon and Salmi the Cobbler') and Esther Hamalkah ('Queen Esther').

Summer Night

Silence is whistling in the open spaces.
A knife in a cat's eye glows.
Night. So much night! In the sky, stillness.
Stars in swaddling clothes.

A wide, wide time. The heart has struck two thousand.
Dew like a rendezvous veils the eyelashes.
Along the pier black slaves fall headlong,
Hurled by lamp's gold lashes.

A summer wind is sailing. Shrouded. Troubled.
Its lips on the shoulders of gardens spilling.
A greenish evil. A seething of lights and suspicion
A treasure in the black froth boiling.

Far on the heights a town, its eyes gold-plated,
with a starved roaring
into stone pillars vaporizes,
dome, spire and tower wrathfully soaring.

Translated by Robert Friend

Tammuz

I go
towards the trumpets of the light,
towards the sun on its summit of rock.
Bright guardian, watch over your flock
lost in the countries of drought.

Boulevards leap in a mane-like blaze.
How shall I raise
my eyes of drunkenness?
The girl of the skies
laughs in her nakedness.
Kiss her. Full on the mouth!

Because of her
the stars at night confound the astronomer.
Because of her
he weeps into his telescope.
I ask for nothing—nothing is my hope.
Therefore is the cyclamen so red
upon the path I tread.

As I step out
upon the empty platform, it is whirled
in glaring, tearing flight,
and I am hurled
heavily to my knees, commanded to cry out
in the multitudinous, deaf-as-thunder light.

Kneel and behold the tints
that set the days aflame,
its dazzling brothers ruling everywhere
when they climb the battlements
with their green braids
and open, like a city, our new day.

My land, the eye must look away
that dares to stare at you.
Like lightning, you reveal
name and place and thing.
No flattering
of voice or shade
has pampered you. The blue
giant has given you all his heart;
the teeth of the gold one hold—
the slaughtering blade.

The silence you have praised, stripped bare,
pierces, like a shriek, the air.
Only when you see your soul a sheep, storm-lost,
do you acknowledge it as yours.

The battles glitter on the distant plain.
The sun will not go out, sky crumple in the dust.
In the far day, a dumbfounded pine
(my emerald soldier!) still runs, attacks, and thrusts.

Translated by Robert Friend

The Olive Tree

Summer has reigned
seventy years;
its mornings have poisoned with avenging light.
The olive tree alone,
my abandoned brother,
has not withdrawn in battle from their brightness.

How holy is its vow, for its black branches
bear neither star nor moon.
Only its poverty, like the Song of Songs, O Earth,
pierces the heart of your stones.

Perhaps from the eyes of its god, its lord,
one tear is granted, heavy and hot,
when like a bookkeeper, breathing anger,
he crouches lonely over your book.

When you wish your mountains to die
and herds bleat for rain and fodder,
it will stand watch on the wall, your solitary bridegroom,
and you will know your life is in its keeping.

And in the evening bleeding with the sunset
it will feel along your face—"Where are you?"...
In its twisted trunk, in the fire of its veins,
it keeps and preserves your tears.

When from the distance the red desert wind
springs violently forth,
it will withdraw
in terror,
for the mountain shall not fall, its heart shall not grow still
so long as one sapling
tears forth from its side.

Translated by Robert Friend

The Third Mother

Mothers are singing. Mothers are singing.
A fist of thunder bangs down.
Strong silence.
Red-bearded lamps are marching
in the empty streets in rows.

Autumn mortally ill, weary, inconsolable autumn,
rain without beginning or end.
No candle in the window, no light in the world,
three mothers
sing.

I hear one of them say:
"He was here but yesterday.
I shall kiss his every fingernail and finger.
I see a tall ship in a calm bay,
and my son from the topmast hanging."

And the second one says:
"My son is tall and quiet.
I am sewing a holiday shirt for my dear.
He's walking in the fields. He will soon be here.
And he holds in his heart a lead bullet."

And the third mother says with her wandering eyes:
No one was dearer or kinder...
"Who shall weep when he comes if I cannot see?
I do not know where he finds him."

And she bathed her eyelashes with weeping.
Perhaps he is only resting.
Perhaps in foreign places
he measures the paths of Your world, O God,
(Like a wandering monk) with kisses.

Translated by Robert Friend

Blood

(FROM "THE TEN PLAGUES")

Naked your night, Amon. The stranger's star a-gleam
Lit up like flame the face of lake and well and stream.
You rose. All was bewitched and like a ruby's fire:
The penny of the poor, the young girl's glowing hair.

A penny of the poor flames like a blood-red eye.
A young girl at the well utters a fearful cry.
She froze, pulled back her hands. "Save me, O God," she cried.
The pail flew down the well until its ringing died.

The blazing red strikes all, whether they wake or sleep.
Her braids, like berry vines, hang down the cistern lip.
Eyelashes are on fire; lips burn, a desert noon.
The son cries out, "O Father"! And he, "My first-born son!"

"My head goes round and round, and yet I did not dance,
And I am parched, dear Father, parched like the desert sands.
O hold me as you did when enemies sacked the City,
And stay me, Father dear, with a water drop of pity.'

"My son, my first-born son, water has turned to blood,
For blood was spilled like water, and poured forth like a flood.
Well waters have grown dark, the eyes of beasts grown red,
For blood was in the City, and the City did not dread."

"There is no end to thirst, no end in all Amon."
"The star of strangers gleams on the City, O my son."
"Father, her waters rise within the pails like fire."
"Her blood is blind, my son, and we are in its power."

Translated by Robert Friend

Hail

(FROM "THE TEN PLAGUES")

...And then the night was shattered. One blow—it reeled and fell!
And then the hail rushed down. A carriage down a hill.
Its heart of darkness torn, how the darkness flared!
To ruin and beauty now the City will be bared.

The living sky poured down, a sky that stones to death.
The ice descending clattered. Hoof beats without a path.
Fire—in the eye of ice. A wounded beast in pain
Totters and charges forward. O sky, strike him again!

Fire—in the eye of ice. That feels no joy nor sorrow.
And silences the cry of the man behind the harrow,
And even when he falls beats him with stone and stone.
The son cries out, "O Father! And he, "My first-born son!"

"The sky's pounced on me, Father, pounced like a beast of prey.
O let the sky like an eagle carry me away.
O feed me to that eagle. And let it dash my brain.
Why are you waiting, Father? Chaos is come again."

"My son, my first-born son, chaos is not yet come.
Here, too, the Law is iron, not pandemonium.
After the kingdom falls (cradle, throne, and shield)—
When the smoke of ruin lifts—the Law shall stand revealed."

"Red as a peony, your life blood dribbles down."
"The Iron Law keeps watch on the City of Amon."
"The smallest of her birds fall wounded in the breast."
"The greatest of her foes have wept and cannot rest."

Translated by Robert Friend

Song to the Wife of My Youth

Not all is vanity, dear,
not all is pride and folly.
I scattered my days to the winds,
I broke my pact with money.
Only you I pursued, my dear,
Like the neck pursues the hangsman.

For you donned your kerchief, dear,
and you asked me to behold you.
And I swore not to taste my bread
till teeth rotted with your unripeness.
I swore to look at you, dear,
till my eyes grew dim with looking.

And sickness struck, my dear,
poverty covered our faces.
And sickness I called "my house,"
and poverty, "our daughter."
We were wretched as dogs, my dear,
and dogs fled from our presence.

Then iron appeared my dear,
beheading me of you
And nothing remained except
my ashes pursuing your shoes.
For iron breaks, my dear,
but my thirst for you is unquenched.

The spirit has no end, my dear;
the body has—and shatters.
Joy did not visit my house
and earth made me a pallet.
But the day you rejoice, my dear,
my dead eyes will rejoice in the darkness.

A day of joy, my dear,
will come and we will share it,
and you'll fall to the earth of my pact
when a coffin rope drops you to me.
Not all is vanity, dear,
not all is pride and folly.

Translated by Robert Friend

The Betrayer

The fallen said, "We are dying."
Those who stumbled said, "We are lost."
But the guilty did not say, "We are guilty."
The betrayer did not say, "I've betrayed."

The betrayer runs to the edge of the field.
Not the living will stone him—the dead will.

In vain he will flee—
The stone is swifter than he.
He turns away his head,
But the stone strikes his head.
The betrayer cries out, "Who's in the field?"
And the stone-hurler cries, "I'm in the field."

And the betrayer will say, "Dead one, return to the dust.
God shows in what befalls you He is just.

For a cry rose from the wall—
You did not say one word.
They tortured your brother behind the wall—
You turned away your head.

O double betrayal,
Heaping with shame
A father's head,
A people's name."

You opened your mouth to assail me with dread.
From you, to the edge of the field I fled,
O Horror in the field, while my face bled.

Who will say, "I died in innocence?"
Who will say, "I was lost but did not sin?"
The guilty will say, "I am guilty."
The betrayer will say, "I betrayed."

The betrayer will say, "I betrayed—
I did not say one word. I was afraid."

Translated by Robert Friend

A Song of Omens

Last night a bird in bitterness cried
  As if hunters hid in the wood;
Last night the glass flew from your hand,
Your dress was ripped as if you had died,
You sat down to sew it, and wearily sighed.
  The needle was covered with blood.

Don't heed the omens, child,
Nor let fear burn in your eyes,
For the omens foretell only good,
For it is joy that knocks on all doors,
And not for you, my child,
But for your torturers.
My child, if dogs weep in the town,
It is an omen, child, of an angel in the town.
If an angel is in the town,
It is an omen, child, of wailing in the town.
Because eyes will grow bright, my child,
And the heavens will curse, my child,
And the years will go by, my child,
And they will remember, my child.
And great omens will be seen,
Nor will they speak in vain,
The humble will rejoice and the poor:
It is joy that knocks on the door.

I am sorry, sorry for your despair
  As if hunters returned from my death.

And I who have no dream, no light
Dreamt you bad dreams at the mouth of the lair;
I woke, and your torn smile grew bright.
   A needle was red in your hand.

Because the language of omens is clear,
Because it speaks in your eye and mine,
Not good is what they foretell,
Not joy will knock on the doors,
And not for you, my child,
But for your torturers.
My child, if dogs weep in the town,
It is an omen, child, of an angel in the town.
An angel in the town
Is an omen that others—you too—
Will perish in the town.
Let your shoulders be ready, my child,
For much is in store, my child,
Without respite to the end, my child,
And an omen will come, my child,
And it will be the last.
You will drink our cup to the end.
To bear these omens—our fate.
My only one, be strong!
Not joy is at the gate.

                    Translated by Robert Friend

As Evening Falls

A vendor of roast chestnuts. He yells by his cart,
Reddening the embers up with a tin fan.
Once covered in Polish soil, and set apart
From the living, he burst out, a living man.

A vintner pours from a keg. He cannot make
His bed until the last late drinker goes:
A vintner who once became a column of smoke
But took a body back and rose.

A blacksmith. Hammer in hand, plying his trade.
Around him sparks of fire flying about.
In the image of a living man he is made
Who with his fist twists the hot iron out.

A minstrel, after lying long on his back,
Rose. Now his innocent tune has found
A circle of listeners, whose limbs were slack
Once, in graves underground.

A waggoner. In a heap of stones was his dying.
He stirred and became alive. He is here today,
Soothing his two white horses down and tying
Their feedbags on in the accustomed way.

A writer whose scattered bones flew into place
And came to life, beyond that rage,
Hunches himself into a little space,
Writing line after line on a long page.

A lover, come back from dust, is also there,
Pausing by a stall or two in the quarter
Where the jewellers are, in search of amber ware
For his wife come back from water.

Amidst fumes of cooking, fumes of soups and stews,
With a charging army of clouds overhead,
So occupied, so practical it is,
So marvellous, the rising of the dead.

Translated by Dom Moraes

The Smithy

The village children hold their breath,
the smith's first hammer blow descending.
So tall the iron sound in the sky,
the mind falls short of comprehending.

The leap and what is leapt for fuse,
sound's birth and life span are a plummet!
The anvil struck, the strong sound soars
beyond return to the sky's summit.

The die once cast, its path ascends
in joy and sorrow—no retreating—
climbing to where the ladder ends
in nothingness, while hearts stop beating.

Till "Hit it hard," the boys cry out,
forestalling the silence of the ages.
The hammer strikes a second blow,
whose sound again time's gear engages.

Translated by Robert Friend

The Foundling

My mother laid me under the wall,
Wrinkled and still, on my back, that night.
I looked up at her as from a well
Till she ran away as one flees from the fight.
I looked up at her as from a well
And the moon was raised over us like a candle.

But slowly, that same night, I rose,
Before the dawn, for the time was fit.
And I returned to my mother's house
As a ball rolls back to the foot that kicked it.
And I returned to my mother's house
And clung to her neck with hands like shadows.

Under God's eye, my mother tore
Me from her neck, like a leech that bit:
But when night returned, I returned as before
And such became our law and habit.
When night returns, I return as before,
And she bows down to the yoke once more.

The doors of her dream are open yet
And only I in that dream can move
For the love of our souls is strung as taut
As a bow, since I first became alive.
For the love of our souls is strung so taut
It can't be sold, it can't be bought.

And therefore God would not separate
Me from my mother's wailing heart.
Once ripped, unweaned, from the breast, I wait.
And from my mother I shall not part.
I enter her house and lock her gate.

She in my prison grew small and spare,
Grew wrinkled in the face like me, grew old.
In white my small hands clothed her
As a mother clothes a living child.
In white my small hands clothed her
And I bore her away without telling her where.

And I laid my mother under the wall,
Watchful and still, on her back, that night.
She looked up laughing as from a well,
And we knew that we had finished the fight.
She looked up laughing as from a well.
The moon was raised over us like a candle.

Translated by Dom Moraes

Antique Song

If you weep in the darkness, I shall light
My sheaves of joy for your sake alone.
If you are chilled to the bone by night,
I will cover you, I will sleep on stone.

If you should wish to dance, one day
I will play for you on my final string.
If you get no presents on your birthday
My death and life, will be what I'll bring.

And if you desire bread or wine,
I, bowed in the back, will see you fed.
I shall bargain away these eyes of mine.
Then I shall buy you both wine and bread.

Yet if once in my absence you should be
Laughing and gay with a chosen few,
The soundless flames of my jealousy
Will burn your roof down over you.

Translated by Dom Moraes

The Maiden

She spun in silence a red thread,
Red as a pomegranate's heart.
The king inside his chamber said:
"She spins me clothes to wear at court".

She spun in silence a black thread,
That darkens day. Far from the king,
The thief locked up in prison said:
"She spins me clothes in which to hang".

She spun in silence a gold thread,
A sword of lightning. On his way,
The harlequin pranced past and said:
"She spins me clothes in which to play".

She spun in silence a grey thread,
The ancestor all colours keep.
The beggar to his mongrel said:
"She spins me clothes in which to weep".

She rose, the coloured threads she took,
And wove them all into a mesh,
And then she went down to the brook,
And there she washed her perfect flesh.

And she put on the woven thing,
And was made beautiful forever:
And she since then is thief and king,
And harlequin and beggar.

Translated by Dom Moraes

LEAH GOLDBERG

1911—

Poet. Born in Kovno, Lithuania, she studied at Lithuanian and German
universities and was awarded a Ph. D. in 1933. Settling in Palestine in
1935, she was literary adviser at the Habima theatre and an editor at
Sifriyat Hapoalim publishing house. She has been lecturer in general literature at the Hebrew University, Jerusalem, since 1954.

Her poems are imbued with a melancholy that is expressed in imagery
and symbols. Marked with delicacy of feeling, they also bear a positive
message that emerges like a flickering ray of light from the surrounding
blackness. Their main themes are wounded love and the yearning for love
and light, tending to aesthetic intellectualism and modernism. Some of her
reminiscent poetry points to a transition from the subjective to the objective.

Her collected poetic works are: Tabaot Ashan ('Smoke Rings'), Shi-
bolet Yerukat ha-Ayin ('Green-Eyed Ear of Corn'), Mi-Beiti ha-Yashan
('From my Old Home'), Al ha-Pericha ('Of Bloom'), Barak BaBoker
('Morning Lightning'), Mukdam u-Meuhar ('Sooner or Later'), Im Ha-
layla Hazeh ('With This Night'). She has written Michtavim Minesia
Meduma ('Letters from an Imaginary Journey') and a lyrical reflective
novel Ve-Hu ha-Or ('And He is the Light'). Her play Ba'alat ha-Armon
('Lady of the Castle') scored a great success in Tel-Aviv. She is also a critic
concerned with literary theory, as in Amanut ha-Sippur ('The Art of Nar-
rative'). She has translated into Hebrew works of Petrarch, Baudelaire,
Verlaine, Ibsen, Rilke, Hoffmansthal, Achmatova, Leo Tolstoy, Alexis
Tolstoy, Chekhov and Mann, and has written poems for children.

Song of the Stream

In the coolness of her dream the stone I kiss
Since I am song and she the silences,
Since I the riddler am, and she the mystery,
And both were formed of one eternity.

The stone I kiss, her solitary face,
And she is faith, and I am who betrays;
The changeless one, creation's secret she,
And I what changes still—discovery.

She is the world; mine is the poet's part:
And time shall tell I touched her silent heart.

Translated by Robert Friend

The Blade of Grass Sings to the River

Even to the children
on the disenchanted shore,
to little ones like me,
one of the myriad poor,
the waters as they rove
murmur, murmur of love.

And when the sun caresses
the stream from time to time,
even I am seen,
where deep the water races,
imaged in the soundless green
where all things are profound.

Deeper grows my image
as seaward it is swirled,
darkens and disappears
on the threshold of forever.
One with the voice of the river,
the murmuring song of the river,
the silent soul declares
the glory of the world.

Translated by Robert Friend

Of Bloom

[I]

The flowering castor, abruptly at night grown dense,
Crimson and warm in leaves that are velvety black.
A line of trees that lean on a barbed wire fence.

The flocks that rested until their limbs were slack
Lag down from the field to the fold. And overhead,
The restless blue shakes a white cloud off its back.

These will fade forever, as lights on the water fade,
But endure in the wild smell of the field and the wood.
At sunset the young grass is soft and red

Almost as if it grew from my still blood.

[II]

An aged woman, sunbronzed, with blue eyes,
Crowned by her suffering and her white hair.
The pail brims silver. From the barndoors rise

Rich vaporous smells that spread across the air.
There is a law of life in her hands milking,
For quiet seamen hold a rope like her.

Here the submissive cows, the unclouded morning.
A woman above flowing white. An ordinary day.
The cloudy secret of a primeval thing,

And the sorceress crouched above her mystery.

Translated by Dom Moraes

Song

I see night stand beyond our window pane,
And—a flower that untimely withers—the white moon wane.
Huge is the childless darkness, huge and wide.
How shall I sing to you, how sit by your side?

Sleep, my sister, my child.
But my sister's eyes stare wild.
In her eyes, as always, appear
The same dream and the fear.
Sleep, my sister, my child.
But my sister's eyes stare wild.

On the doorstep of our house you sat and wept
As the sun wearily from dawn to evening crept.
On the doorstep of our house you wept the whole day long.
There is left us only this one song:

Sleep, sister, and forget.
My sister's eyes are wet.
In her eyes as always, appear
The same dream and the fear.
Sleep, my sister, sleep.
The eyes of my sister weep.

At the window of our house gray grows the light;
The song will end with the watch at the end of night.
The whole world listens at the break of day.
Silent we shall return who silent went away.

Sleep, my sister, my child.
My sister's eyes stare wild.

Translated by Robert Friend

The Thorn

How it dares on the parched earth,
Upon the rock and sand
To flower, to burst forth and flower,
Laying down the law of this land.

Unyielding and proud and austere
It blooms like a pitiless flame.
The thorn in the desert stands,
A prophet who uncovers your shame.

Translated by Robert Friend

Twenty Years Later

[I]

Now it is twenty years; and, as one says,
"Something has touched the world in which we live".
This feeling's not rare wine, preserved long days.
It gains no body, nor does it improve.

Believe me, it is not your snowy hair;
Only perhaps your cool indifferent smile—
The scrolls of both our lives are hidden there,
And what has "touched the world" in the meanwhile.

Two people: yes: there are two strangers here,
Who spanned the abyss of terror and decay,
And even by the graves of those once dear,
It is a different prayer we shall say.

[II]

A flock of years that prays.
Legions of white days.
A flock of years that prays:
All turned to desert sand.

For God's sake don't begin
To portion out the sin.
Always it is your sin,
And sinful here I stand.

Time lies between us, dead.
Blood of his years was shed.
Time, our loved one, dead.
May earth receive his bones...

On each side we stand chilled
Like foes who quit the field.
Our dead lie in the field
And nobody atones.

Translated by Dom Moraes

Antigone

[I]

Try to rest. And try to sleep.
That's how it is. This is what you were promised.
Not a betrayal. The truth was printed deep
On tablets of the earth your foot once kissed.

Tomorrow. Tomorrow. The dawn of the dead
Drowned under birdcalls: but the others, those
Left in the city, laboured on for bread
In market, roadway, house.

But only you among the tombs were walking.
Only to you they forecast Judgment Day.
You will bear witness then to everything.
Now it is in this world that you must pay.

But all the world is still. Even your dead
No longer wish to hear from you. So try
And sleep: or in the meantime rest instead.
Rest on your fate, rest peacefully.

[II]

No rain will fall. Clouds loll
On the horizon like dead witnesses
Whom nobody will call.
Smug people in the city leave their houses.

Hundreds of brothers there, who watched the dawn
Of death, you recognise. But look, they move,
Drifting past you, forgetful, and are gone.
For the time being, they also need to live.

No rain will fall. The dry
Soil expects nothing now, numbed by the years
Of strangling; of memory flying by;
Of silence; of your silent tears.

No rain will fall. Everything has come true.
Try to live without this storm in you.

Translated by Dom Moraes

Song of the Strange Woman

[I]

I am green and replete like a song that has blown through the grass,
I am deep and soft as a bird-nest,
I come from yesterday,
from the forest that taught me to breathe,
from the well where I drank of the light,
from the exhausted lovers embraced and sleeping in the grass.

I am from there,
from the village of the small winds,
from skies that weave low clouds with bluish smoke.
I hear your voices still,
blue as your smoke and dim.
I come from the village of clattering wooden spoons.
I am from there.

[II]

Windmill, windmill,
on what shore did the gulls cry
the name of my dead land?
Windmill, windmill.

On what street did they walk
who did not turn their heads,
the kingdom of the sunset on their backs?
And the wings whirred in the wind.

] 423 [

Where?
Is the garden there, crimson
with autumn, burying shadows,
hiding the twilights under the leaves;
making way, making way for the wind?

And the wind, did they cry and the gull—
the name of my dead land?
Windmill, windmill!

[III]

Land of low clouds, I belong to you.
I carry in my heart your every drop of rain.
On stumbling feet, without an angel to lean on, I travel towards you,
bringing mushrooms of your forest to the kingdom of heaven.

In the kingdom of heaven, they still remember your feast day.
A gay harmonica is playing the song of the dead.
And a star entangled in the arms of the wind.
is turning, turning—
and I have grown old, grown gray, and who will dance with me?

Nevertheless, for the gate is open there,
I shall be at the festival:
I shall take off my shoes and sit down in the shade.
Slowly my face will float on a lazy stream,
my face lit up by the rivers
of your remembered shores.
Windmill, windmill!

Translated by Robert Friend

GAVRIEL PREIL

1911—

Poet. Born in Estonia, he has been living in the United States since 1922.

His poems indicate a profound sensitivity to landscape and its changing shades and colours; they portray the struggles of the poet in the throes of creation, alive to the problems of the modern world, which totters on the brink of extinction.

His collected poems have been published under the titles: Nof ve-Shemesh u-Kefor *(' Scenery and Sun and Frost'),* Ner Mul Kochavim *('Candle against the Stars'),* Mapat Erev *('Map of Evening').*

] 425 [

A Small, Proud Autumn

Strange how with the chestnuts warming up my pocket
I have become the bearer of a small, brown autumn.
I am independent now,
Untempted by the snares that a praised season
lay at my feet; free of the wonders
of vapour and of crystal
that covered the land so quickly.

Strange how with the chestnuts warming up my pocket
I have grown proud like one
unsheathing a brown loneliness,
who finds it now abounds with buds of fresh, new colours
that the great autumn does not know.

Perhaps because of this I suddenly saw a king
burning with despair and plundered of a crown.

Translated by Robert Friend

Concerning the Cherry Tree

[I]
The cherry tree is red again
and the old man
who let me taste of it last year
is gone.
His fruit is darker now.
My fruit grows darker, too.

[II]
Whether the tree has felt
the old man's absence
I do not know,
but this is clear: this year its fruit ascend
in a rebellious, roaring conflagration
proclaiming against death's night
life's repeating colours.
May the ultimate storm,
the one that cleans our bones,
be like the summer
that makes a seething sea
of the gold of its glory forever.

Translated by Robert Friend

New York

Half-past eleven. A hot day floats like a wave, burns like a forest.
Before me the city, like one inviting seduction, strips like a desert.
My eyes are red with a restless night, my mouth tastes sand and
    weariness,
and I am like a beast trapped by a dazzler
who beats on the panes as on the drums of Tophet;
a hunter whose poison bullets shoot from savannahs of boredom.

Soon in her different summer comes a woman—
with peaches, small, cool suns in the bounds of a green platter;
her smooth arms flowing—peaceful streams.
Afterwards we shall arrive where sea-tongues lap the shore,
and the fire of the day will die.

Translated by Robert Friend

Rains on the Island

After the first sudden rain,
the long pause after,
fleets of water anchored once again
before the window,
and we were like sad sailors of the dusk,
forsaken of all ports.

At home the coffee that we drank was bitter-hot
like the onslaught of the spring.
The bread we ate was good upon the tongue
as if the meadow-scent were in our nostrils.
The summer soon will knock upon our doors—
and we shall be
sailors of the dusk
drinking in its golden showers,
but sadder still.

Translated by Robert Friend

Words of Oblivion and Peace

To Jenny N.

I once broke evening bread with the brown-faced, white-smiled
    Prince of Siam.
He wore festivity and humility as the first skin of his body.
His talk touched on London and New York—large villages lacking
    true wonders,
and his memory dwelt on the people of his country, small of
    stature, eaters of pale rice,
and on the flowers there, high-tide huge, and summoning, ablaze,
    the armies of their colours.
Lowering his low voice, "There is nothing," he said, "like the
absolute oblivion that Buddha gives.
No smallest eddy will ever ruffle its seas,
and there is nothing like the calm of the endless seasons
    that dream in its orchards."

Suddenly, a wind blew from the corner of the street, a prayer spoke
    from beyond the bridges
but as the flesh grew sad and silent in its fated valleys,
through the window-pane there poured a peach and northern sunset,
and I saw Jenny, the villages of her peaceful words in flower.

Translated by Robert Friend